D0058214

DATE DUE

DEMCO 38-296

A Larger Sense of Purpose

The 2003 Clark Kerr Lectures

A Larger Sense of Purpose

HIGHER EDUCATION
AND SOCIETY

❖

HAROLD T. SHAPIRO

PRINCETON UNIVERSITY PRESS

PRINCETON AND OXFORD

Riverside Community College
AUG '06 Library
4800 Magnolia Avenue
Riverside, CA 92506

LC 191.94 .S43 2005

Shapiro, Harold T., 1935–

A larger sense of purpose

Copyright © 2005 by Princeton University Press

⌐n University Press, 41 William Street,
⌐on, New Jersey 08540
⌐gdom: Princeton University Press,
⌐oodstock, Oxfordshire OX20 1SY
⌐l Rights Reserved

⌐ss Cataloging-in-Publication Data

⌐ro, Harold T., 1935–
⌐ose : higher education and society :
non nobis solum / Harold T. Shapiro.
p.   cm.
"The 2003 Clark Kerr lectures."
Includes bibliographical references and index.
ISBN-13: 978-0-691-12363-9 (cloth : alk. paper)
ISBN-10: 0-691-12363-2 (cloth : alk. paper)
1. Education, Higher—Social aspects—United States. 2. Education,
Higher—Aims and objectives—United States. 3. Education, Higher—
United States—History. I. Title.
LC191.94.S43   2005
306.43′2—dc22   2005043381

British Library Cataloging-in-Publication Data is available

This book has been composed in Sabon

Printed on acid-free paper. ∞

pup.princeton.edu

Printed in the United States of America

1   3   5   7   9   10   8   6   4   2

Riverside Community College
Library
1800 Magnolia Avenue
Riverside, CA 92503

Non nobis solum *

❖

* Loosely translated as "not for ourselves alone"

❖ *Contents* ❖

❖ *Prologue* ❖

I T I S A SPECIAL honor to have been chosen to give the first in what will be a series of biannual lectures established to honor Clark Kerr, the very memorable president of the University of California. In the fifteen years he served first as chancellor of the Berkeley campus (1952–1958) and then as president of the University of California (1958–1967), he stood at the center of an institution characterized, somewhat paradoxically, by both great conflict and increasing academic distinction. An unkind and uninformed observer might characterize his tenure as chancellor and then president as bracketed by the aftermath of the loyalty oath controversy in the early years and by the Free Speech Movement in his last years. The fact is that despite these controversies, some of which were externally driven, he never lost sight of the big picture. His stubborn dedication to the possibilities that lay ahead were a key factor in enabling the Berkeley campus and the University of California to move from strength to strength.

One of the ironies of the tenure of this thoughtful Quaker was that at various times he was denounced enthusiastically by both the political left and the political right. He must have been doing something right! He certainly had the courage to offend many powerful people in defense of what he thought was right not only relative to his own beliefs, but in the long term interests of the university he served. The 1960 Master Plan alone would have been sufficient to establish him as an innovative builder of American higher education, but his contributions went far beyond that both in his years at California and subsequently. In my judgment, President Kerr's record as an innovator, a continuing source of inspiration and as the builder of a great institution is unquestionable. While controversy often raged about him, whether about which political views were too dangerous to be spoken on campus or whether he had mounted a sufficient defense of academic values against what many thought were the corrosive attitudes of certain members of the state legislature and/or of the university's regents, he never lost sight of the university's long-term goals and aspirations. Further, he had the moral courage, good humor, and humility to make thoughtful compromises in the service of these goals and to forgive many of his less thoughtful critics. Clark Kerr realized that important human and academic values could be at odds with one another and that one must always confront the moral complexities of life.

Like all truly great educators within a liberal society, Kerr considered the future to be a carrier of even greater possibilities and, therefore, to be of ethical significance. As a leader he took risks both to safeguard an institution and to provide for its future. His experience reminds us all of the need to defend the intellectual independence of the university. Leadership requires fighting many battles, even those battles where one expects a momentary defeat.

Michael Walzer (1994) has pointed out that our particular version of liberal politics has been carefully developed over a long period of time through a series of overlapping, complex, and often controversial social and political negotiations. Clark Kerr believed that one of the university's responsibilities in such a context was not only to participate but to ensure that the articulation and nourishment of the aspirations of higher education remained a part of the broader national discourse.

By his example, Clark Kerr reminded us that our national discourse should be not only thoughtful, but characterized by both the intellectual discipline and the intellectual and moral imagination that sustain and constrain each other. Furthermore, he had the humility to understand that those with different opinions were not necessarily the enemy, but part of a common moral community searching for the best way to make this a better world.

I want also to comment briefly on Clark Kerr's ideas regarding the relationships among the wide variety of universities, colleges, community colleges, and research universities that together constitute American higher education. President Kerr had the good sense to honor each of these for the distinctive contributions they make to our national life, and the wisdom to realize the benefits of sustaining a heterogeneous system that would meet the manifold needs of our nation, the worlds of education and scholarship, and the full spectrum of the nation's high school and college graduates. This particular perspective helped make possible the distinctive structure and extraordinary distinction of the higher education sector in California in the second half of the twentieth century. I believe that jurisdictions outside of California would be well served to follow policies that reflect this aspect of Clark Kerr's vision.

Judging from both his actions and his words, I think that President Kerr also believed, as I do, that the nature of the contemporary American university is deeply connected to and formed by our particular version of liberal democracy, most especially by our commitments to equal opportunity, to a certain discomfort with the status quo, and to the liberal desire to create a better world by finding better structures and arrangements for all that we think and do. His voice of reason and logic was also a voice of conviction and passion that has provoked me and many others to sustain the intellectual energy and moral direction to do better things.

For these and many other reasons, I join a virtual army of persons who continue to be fascinated by his experience as president of the University of California, to forgive his errors and to admire his many contributions to the worlds of scholarship and education and to our nation. It would be quite impossible to do justice to Clark Kerr's legacy within the scope of this year's series of lectures. But I am certainly grateful to be associated with his name and his broad interests in higher education and society through this lectureship. Over time I hope the Kerr lectures will not only remind us of how much President Kerr contributed to higher education and the society it serves, but also deepen our understanding of the relationship between higher education and society.

All social institutions exist in some state of symbiosis with the society of which they are a part. This assertion is simply to acknowledge that each institution has its role to play, its responsibilities to perform and, most revealing, its just desserts to receive. Its just desserts, of course, will reflect a great deal about the value society places on the institution's contribution to the culture. However, societies and their myriad of social institutions and cultural norms are always a project under construction. Each institution both adapts to its environment and helps alter that environment. Like individual members within a given biological species, particular institutions within a certain sector may vary a good deal in their distinctive set of assets, their environment, and their capacity to branch out in new directions. Thus, in American higher education a great variety of colleges and universities participate in the ongoing construction of our joint future. There is a limit, of course, to the diversity of structures and forms that can be accommodated. In most eras the ascendancy of particular values is reflected in one way or another in the evolving structure and programs of most educational institutions. At any moment, however, a particular type of institution may be performing a central and very valuable role, or exist more or less on the periphery of things, largely ignored by the forces driving society forward.

Although the Western university is often characterized as one of the few institutions that have survived since medieval times, its form, relevance, social role(s), and just desserts have changed so greatly that the resemblance of the contemporary research university to its medieval counterpart, or to the even earlier Islamic institutions of higher education, is that of a rather distant descendants. From our current vantage point, where the university is such a central actor in supplying so many of the key ingredients now required by all "advanced" societies, it is difficult to recall that for most of the period between the twelfth century and now, the university was a rather marginal institution. Indeed as one considers the broad history of institutions of higher education since medieval times, one is forced to bear witness to numerous periods of decline and intellectual dreariness. During other periods, however, the university has been the home of important intellectual developments in learning and scholarship. In such times the relationship between university and society becomes much more salient, to the point where the very nature of the interactions between university and society have been fundamentally transformed. These periods of critical reexamination of the university's role and the nature of its educational and scholarly agenda have been key to its social survival and evolution. At the same time, they have moved the university farther and farther from its medieval counterpart, creating the rather tenuous connection between today's research universities and their twelfth-century ancestors. Our continuing affection for the medieval university is partly symbolic and partly nostalgic. For us it represents the renewed flourishing of scholarship, a new openness, a common language (Latin) and religion (Catholicism), and a certain independence that we continue to admire and, at times, long for.

In view of the extraordinary pace of change in our society and around the globe, there are pressures on all institutions to change and adapt. In such an environment it is more essential than ever for the community of universities to define well its set of values and the sense of purpose that guides its efforts. Otherwise we risk being either overwhelmed by values and commitments that are inimical to the world of scholarship and learning, or caught up both in the rampant materialism of our age and the incentive structure of private markets. In this latter respect, I believe that universities would be well advised to acknowledge both the virtues and the limitations of market incentives as they apply to the enterprise of education and scholarship. Although under a broad variety of circumstances private markets remain an extraordinarily efficient means for mobilizing resources and for the efficient production and distribution of goods and services, they are not always effective in dealing with the issues of social and economic justice that are so central to higher education's role, or in mobilizing resources for long-term risky ventures whose outcomes not only are speculative, but cannot be controlled or privatized. The market is not the only social institution we need to ensure the flourishing of humankind.

The subject of the lectures that follow is the nature of the contemporary relationship between the university and society. Although one of the lectures deals with historical issues, the principal focus is on certain contemporary issues and challenges as society's circumstance, goals, and aspirations change and as America's colleges and universities consider taking on a variety of new tasks, assuming new social roles, and at times ponder an almost complete restructuring of their organizations.

I begin this volume with an outline of my own views regarding the dynamic relationship between the university and society. In particular, I focus on the challenges presented by the increased commercialization of both the principal products of the university, namely, education and the development of new knowledge, and of what many consider to be an activity on the periphery of university life, intercollegiate athletics. In the second essay, titled "The Transformation of the Antebellum College: From Right Thinking to Liberal Learning," I address the question of why the Colonial or antebellum college lasted so long, and I try to understand those aspects of its eventual transformation that can be traced to the contingencies of the post–Civil War period that generated the distinctly American aspects of the contemporary university.

In my third essay I address the evolving nature and role of a liberal arts education and its relation to liberal democracy, the relationship between the faculties of the arts and sciences and professional schools, and finally, the university's continuing responsibilities, if any, for moral education. And in my fourth essay I address the set of issues that surround the university's role in the scientific enterprise and some of its ethical, moral, and cultural implications.

There are, of course, many other important challenges facing American higher education in the coming decades that I will not touch on in these lectures. These include the ongoing revolution in information technology, which may or may not sweep all before it but will continue to have a significant impact on many aspects of the university's teaching and research program. Another formidable challenge that I want to acknowledge but will not address in these lectures is the ability of universities to continue to select a socially desirable and competitive configuration of programs while maintaining a commitment consistent with its role as social critic to stand at an angle to society. This latter challenge often emerges in the public's awareness as an issue of costs. It has always been my position, however, that the basic underlying issue with respect to costs is whether society believes, given its investment, that the university is generating adequate social dividends. Another way to articulate this issue is to ask whether universities are efficiently producing the right programs. In this respect there is a useful analogy to the current controversy over health care costs. I have always thought that it is not the level of costs per se that is bothering people; it is whether or not they feel that they are getting their money's worth, or whether there are unaddressed issues of social justice in the distribution of health services. The same set of concerns is behind the controversy over the costs of higher education.

Throughout these lectures I will return again and again to both the ethical challenges faced by academic communities and to considerations of the central political and cultural commitments of liberal societies, because these factors play a vital role in our conceptions and expectations of our universities. In particular, I hope that an examination of these matters will help us understand the nature of the research university as a public trust, or an institution with a public purpose, and, therefore, recognize the constantly changing character of its social responsibilities. I have chosen to focus on these issues because I believe that the future of the research university is dependent on the nature of the values and objectives informing the university's leadership at all levels. Most of all it depends on a vision of who we are and what we would like to become. It depends on understanding, for example, what we as a university would not allow ourselves to do even if offered additional resources; what we would do with or without additional resources; and what we would do only if additional resources are made available. In short, it depends on having a well-understood and socially compelling sense of purpose. Without such a vision or sense of purpose, or antecedent set of commitments, the university, for better or worse, will simply be swept along either by the ever more aggressive materialistic forces in our society, the demands of individuals dominated by a narrow concern with their self-fulfillment, and/or other forces and institutions with neither the will nor the interest to nourish the intellectual and educational values of the world of scholarship and education. Even children realize that the fulfillment of their material desires, important as it is, is not sufficient to realize their humanity. Amassing resources, knowledge, and wisdom is not enough. We must also have some compelling notions regarding how this growing patrimony is to be deployed. To avoid disappointment, we have to know what would disappoint us! Only with such knowledge will we be prepared to fight for what we believe in, even if some of these battles may be lost. Only then will we be ready to act as if taking risks for our beliefs is essential for our survival.

A Larger Sense of Purpose

The University and Society

We can and must help create a better world, but every opportunity pursued involves a wager on the future.

IN CHOOSING as the title of this volume *A Larger Sense of Purpose: Higher Education and Society*, I meant to convey the notion that universities, like other social institutions and even individuals, ought to serve interests that include but move beyond narrow self-serving concerns. The epigraph of this volume, the Latin phrase *non nobis solum*, "not for ourselves alone," echoes this thought. To my regret, this is one of those ideas that, while applauded in principle, is easily lost in the challenge of meeting one's day-to-day responsibilities. This makes it even more important to pause once in a while to adjust our sails and correct our course.

PUBLIC AND PRIVATE UNIVERSITIES

All higher education institutions, both public and private, both nonprofit and for-profit, and from state colleges to research universities to community colleges to a wide variety of technical and professional schools, serve a public purpose. Considerable variation in quality, purpose, and aspirations exists in each of these sectors. Nevertheless, they each play a distinctive and important role. The resulting heterogeneity of America's institutions of higher education not only matches the wide spectrum of achievement and aspiration of entering students, but is one of the principal sources of strength and vitality of American higher education. The opportunity for Americans to more fully realize their educational aspirations through a variety of paths and at a number of different points in their life cycle is an important and distinctive aspect of American higher education. The idea

1

that all young people develop in lockstep, so that at age eighteen we can sort this age cohort into their final positions within the educational opportunity system, runs counter to everything we know about human development and early childhood experience. The American system of higher education offers an unusually large variety of entry points, relatively speaking, to the so-called elite programs. If you do not do so well in high school, you can begin at a community college, but if you do well enough there you can transfer to an excellent university, and if you do well enough there you can participate in a distinguished graduate or professional program. Moreover, there is a healthy flow of human capital and ideas among these sectors. As a result, maintaining strength and quality in each of higher education's sectors contributes to the strength of every component of the system. In my judgment it would be a mistake for each of these different sectors to lose their distinctiveness by, for example, becoming too much like one another or trying to emulate the so-called elite institutions. Although this tendency is understandable, I believe it should be resisted as a matter of public policy at both the state and the federal level.

Indeed, given the increasing globalization of our social, cultural, economic, and political environment, the quality of American higher education depends not only on sustaining its heterogeneity, but also on the strength and vitality of institutions of higher education elsewhere, which have their own distinctive approaches. The American university continues to be enriched by the flow of talent and ideas from abroad, and it increasingly depends on it, just as talent and ideas from abroad increasingly depend on us. The health and vitality of American higher education will remain unfulfilled if our counterparts abroad are not prospering.

In these lectures, however, I will focus primarily on the American research university, because this is an area of higher education in which I have spent my entire academic career and to which I have given my most careful consideration. Within this sector, however, I will not distinguish between the private and public research universities because their differences, which are significant, are not central to the particular issues I have chosen to address. My view is that despite some significant contrasts, private and public research universities have an enormous amount in common. Most important, they are members of a common educational and scholarly community. Moreover, they are quite dependent on one another, and faculty, students, ideas, and even academic resources move quickly and relatively freely among them. For the most part, faculty and students who move from one to the other can adapt easily because the basic nature of their work will be largely unaffected. Though senior administrative officials need to relate to somewhat different constituencies, many constituencies, such as students, faculty, alumni, and the federal government, are the same. Of course, one key difference is the special relationship of university officials and trustees of public universities with state government officials.

As I reflect on my own experience first as president of the University of Michigan and then at Princeton, many obvious distinctions come to mind—their differences in size, their relative commitments to professional education, their different but overlapping constituencies. Less noticed, but equally important and interesting, were two important distinctions relating to presidential leadership and overall governance. For the president of a flagship state university such as the University of Michigan, a constant challenge was to convince those groups with political influence in the state (e.g., legislators and governors, various unions, important corporate interests, etc.) not only that their interests and the university's interests overlapped at least somewhat, but that the university had legitimate objectives of its own that they should recognize and support because these interests also served the citizens of the state. As a result, the university's objectives and exactly what the university was and who it should serve were always in the process of negotiation.

At Princeton the analogous challenge of mobilizing the university's constituencies was somewhat different. By and large, the broader Princeton community shared a common set of objec-

3

tives. Thus the board's discussions—or any intrauniversity negotiations—were more likely to focus on strategy as opposed to
objectives. On the governance front, there were at least two interesting differences. First, Michigan's regents were elected in
partisan statewide elections, whereas Princeton's were either
elected by the alumni body or selected by the board itself. Second, the Michigan board met in public. In both cases, many dedicated and thoughtful persons came to occupy seats on the governing board. However, the Michigan board's public meetings
often provided a venue or platform for the discussion of largely
irrelevant but popular public issues and causes that became con-
fused with university business and priorities. Ironically, that
meant that, in order to avoid certain public discussion, and as
long as a certain level of trust existed between the board and the
president, the Michigan board was more likely to delegate its
authority to the president.

Trust between the president and the governing board is an
essential ingredient in achieving the potential of any American
university or college. The establishment and maintenance of this
trust is the responsibility of the president and is primarily an
educational function. In this respect it is important to acknowledge that although final authority over all matters rests with the
board, the board's responsibility is to use this authority wisely.
The board may indeed be in charge, but they are in charge of an
institution that serves a public purpose. Presidents must also act
judiciously, but any time they believe that board actions present
a serious threat to the institution's informing values, they must
say so publicly.

Finally, I return to the two most critical characteristics that
public and private universities share: they serve society as both
a responsive servant and a thoughtful critic. Thus, although the
modern research university must serve society by providing the
educational and other programs in high demand, the university
must also raise questions that society does not want to ask and
generate new ideas that help invent the future, at times even

"pushing" society toward it. In this latter respect the contemporary research university is a prototypical liberal institution, always looking for a better set of arrangements within a wide spectrum of our individual and community lives. These two roles define the nature of the university's public trust, whether it is a public or private institution. In fact, many public universities have been rapidly privatizing some of their programs in the sense of substituting federal resources, private giving, and tuition revenues for state subsidies. This process, especially marked in areas of professional education such as law and business, has narrowed even further the difference between public and private research universities. We deployed this strategy among others in dealing with the financial crisis we faced in the early 1980s at the University of Michigan, although we seldom referred to it in these terms. Certainly, it was not our preferred path, but it was one line of attack within a broader overall program aimed at sustaining the quality of our programs.

Although public and private research universities meet their various obligations in somewhat different fashions, they share the same central responsibilities as public trusts. The idea of the public trust, in somewhat different form, preceded the research university. For example, in 1833, Harvard's president, Josiah Quincy, in an appeal to the legislature of Massachusetts, made a point of emphasizing the public character of Harvard's library assets while the relevant senate committee, in response to his petition, referred to the Corporation of Harvard University as trustees for the public interest. The character or shape of this public trust will change over time. It is shaped most importantly by the public policies, cultural and political traditions, and legal framework of the liberal democracy of which colleges and universities are a part. Thus, when we think about the priorities of the research university we must be attentive not only to its special privileges, from its intellectual and educational autonomy to its special tax status, but also to its public obligations. A private university such as Princeton is not some kind of private social club conferring benefits, earned or unearned, on its members. The major decisions of private universities must take the public interest into account. Princeton, for example, needs to be continually conscious of how much of its assets, all of which exist to serve a public purpose, should be distributed for the benefit of the current faculty and student body, and how much should be preserved for future generations. The answer to this question should depend, in significant measure, on how this decision will help the university meet its public obligations. For example, it may depend on how accessible the university is currently to talented young people across all socioeconomic classes.

More important, all research universities, public or private, must constantly reevaluate whose interests are being served by their current policies and programs. Everyone's interests cannot be served at the same time. At Princeton, for example, our most significant initiatives in financial aid and enrollment were driven by just such an examination of the status quo ante. We came to believe that in order to more fully meet our public purpose, we would need to dramatically expand our student financial aid program, substitute grants for loans, make our full financial aid program available to students from abroad, and provide additional opportunity through a modest expansion of our undergraduate enrollment. At Michigan during the difficult financial times of the early 1980s, our judgment was that we could best meet our public obligations by focusing on sustaining the quality of our programs, even at the cost of offering fewer programs. This judgment may or may not have been correct, but we approached the challenge in that spirit. Other institutions with their own distinctive traditions, resources, and aspirations, but facing similar or different challenges, might select quite different initiatives to meet their responsibilities as a public trust. Thus, although financial aid at Princeton is 100 percent need-based, many other research universities, both public and private, believe, quite appropriately, that some merit scholarships are essential to fulfilling their public responsibilities.

6

THE DYNAMIC RELATIONSHIP BETWEEN
UNIVERSITIES AND SOCIETY

It is hardly surprising that Western higher education has transformed itself and its relationship to society a number of times over the last millennium, given that society's view of itself has also been transformed many times during this same period. A crisis in education is usually caused by a crisis in society that calls into question many existing ideas regarding the central issues of knowledge, culture, and society. The crisis fuels *meaningful* educational debates and propels changes in educational institutions such as universities. By *meaningful debates* I mean debates that lead to significant changes in the curriculum. Too often, long, drawn-out, and even bitter debates leave little trace on the learning experience of students. We often forget that it is not our internalized ideas regarding what we teach that matters, but what students learn, what they come to care about, and what they themselves become.

In a rapidly changing world, the social role and form of the university and its programs exist in an almost perpetual state of transition facing constant challenges of leadership and adaptability. For example, the future role of the university will depend, in part, on the particular shape taken by our evolving liberal democracy. Will democracy evolve by focusing its efforts on individual choice and open access, or on the direct provision of economic and social benefits of one kind or another? Alternatively, will our politics focus on trying to find a new position of political equipoise between group and individual rights? Or will the evolving policies of our government focus on the new moral, social, economic, and political issues that globalization is now putting before us? Clearly, many other foci and/or combinations of foci are possible within a broadly liberal democratic form of government. Moreover, it remains to be seen whether the notion that scientific progress will bring progress in other dimensions of the human endeavor such as ethics and political arrangements

7

has any lasting vitality. Although I acknowledge the possibility, I do not in these pages consider the more sobering challenge that liberal democracy, in combination with modern capitalism and modern technology, eventually causes a nation to lose its soul and slide into some form of tyranny within an autocratic state. The key point is that public policies and priorities have an impact on universities. In these essays I have assumed not only that liberal politics will survive, but that whatever its future path, our particular version of liberal politics will continue to have a decisive influence on key aspects of American higher education. Needless to say, the impetus for change in higher education may also be internal, arising from developments on the scholarly and educational frontier.

In contemporary times, a university education is almost a requirement of a fully expressed citizenship. The university is an essential supplier of products and services on which the society is highly dependent, such as advanced training, expertise of various types, and new ideas. However, the capacity of the university as we know it to maintain such a central role will always remain uncertain and depends on the university's adaptability, its capacity for leadership, and the evolving nature of other key cultural and political ideas and institutions. The difficulty is that change and adaptation inevitably bring in their wake anxiety, loss, and controversy. Meaningful change generates not only winners and losers, but also a reconfiguration of the values and commitments of the university. There are always constituencies, internal and external, that think that the existing configuration is optimal. Thus, even thoughtful change creates controversy. It always requires courage and commitment from within the university leadership, whether at a department, a school, or a university. At the same time, errors are certain when selecting new paths, and leaders need both the courage to take risks and the wisdom to identify when a mistake has been made. Making the right choices in higher education is something like trying to understand which aspects of avant-garde art are simply different and transitory, and which aspects represent a more permanent addition to our cultural patrimony.

I recall with mixed feeling two initiatives, one at Princeton and one at Michigan. In the late 1970s and the early 1980s, as Michigan's manufacturing sector faltered (after the "second energy shock"), the state of Michigan and the University of Michigan faced a serious financial crisis. At the University of Michigan we developed a response to this situation that could be loosely characterized as "smaller but better." The idea was that, given external circumstances, the only way we could continue to enhance the quality of our programs was to have fewer of them. This involved both dropping our commitments to some perfectly reasonable and worthy activities and increasing our commitments to others. Although the general strategy was widely accepted in principle, it was extremely difficult to implement because few members of our community thought that they would be personally affected. When particular decisions were made there was fierce resistance among those negatively affected and little support from the strategy's beneficiaries. In time, however, this approach was widely appreciated by most, but on a personal level it would have been much easier for leadership at all levels to simply let the average quality of our programs slowly diminish.

At Princeton in the early 1990s I began to think that, in order to sustain the quality of the undergraduate experience, we should increase the number of undergraduates from abroad. The reasons: increased globalization and the fact that many Princeton students had their first postgraduation experience abroad. Increasing the number of students from abroad would, in our judgment, improve the undergraduate experience for all our students. The vehicle we chose to accomplish this was to continue our competitive admissions process but fully open our financial aid program to students from abroad. Harvard had had such a practice for many years. The idea was immediately popular with our faculty and students, but because we were about to launch a capital campaign I went around the country explaining the idea to our alumni. The reaction was bimodal. Some thought such an initiative self-evident and overdue and offered to help by providing new endowments for the purpose. Others, however, became outraged, arguing that too many deserving American students might be deprived or that we could not get reliable financial information for our need-based financial aid program. The debate quickly became polarized. We decided, therefore, to approach our new objective in steps and see what happened. In the end, our alumni widely accepted the program but not before considerable acrimony and accusations of various sorts passed under the bridge.

At its best the contemporary American research university is a much more audacious idea than the Colonial college. It is a place where learning, knowledge, skills, and traditions are preserved, reevaluated, and transmitted; where new ideas, scholars, and teachers are born; and where interests and cultural commitments of all kinds meet and inform one another. From a more historical perspective, it is a place where the achievements, hopes, and interests of our recovered past meet and interact with those of the present as we shape our cultural traditions for the future. The contemporary research university, therefore, can also be thought of as holding a continuing conversation with both past and future generations regarding those matters that are truly significant.

In prosaic terms the three principal tasks of the university are the preservation, transmission, and advancement of knowledge. These tasks and the freedom to interpret what they mean, however, are always in transition. At times the university's social role has been to serve as a bastion of the status quo and a defender of the interests and values of those currently in power. The medieval university, for example, after a relatively brief period of independence, quickly became captive to the interests of the church and ruling elites, although there were always some heroic souls who fought for the application of independent logical analysis in matters of scholarship. Their programs, attitudes, and commitments fully reflected this subservient status. To some extent the same could be said of America's Colonial colleges. At other times, however, universities have been a force for change, playing a significant role in society's critical self-examination, helping to allow a shift in the allocation of resources and power. In these moments the university becomes a truly liberal and liberated institution. This was true, for example, for certain German universities during the first half of the nineteenth century and has been increasingly true of the American research university in the post–World War II era.

In retrospect, it is quite startling how effectively the Colonial colleges, the early land grant universities, and other entirely new private institutions such as Johns Hopkins, Stanford, Chicago, and Cal Tech mobilized themselves in the later nineteenth century to provide an ever broader set of services. They expanded and redefined undergraduate education and moved quickly to monopolize a good deal of advanced professional education, becoming barely a half-century later key components of the nation's research and development enterprise. None of these developments was preordained. Indeed, American higher education on the eve of the Civil War seemed an unlikely foundation for such developments. Left to their own devices without the strong leadership of the newer institutions, it is unlikely that the Colonial colleges would have responded in such an agile and imperialistic fashion.

For the foreseeable future, existing colleges and universities will be faced with the challenge of sustaining society's most important values, demonstrating sufficient adaptability to fill new and/or modified roles, and exerting sufficient leadership to help society shape new cultural commitments and expand others. Although this portfolio of responsibilities represents a significant challenge for faculty, administrators, and trustees, a great deal is at stake, namely, the continued social relevance of institutions of higher education. If such leadership should falter, it would not be the first time that a significant social institution was replaced, in whole or in part, by other institutions better able to articulate and meet society's evolving needs. Will the current American research university have the will and the courage to

11

respond as thoughtfully to the changes that are surely ahead of us? Within universities the forces protecting the status quo are always strong and ready with a portfolio of reasons why change is too risky. The more distinguished the university, the stronger these forces. However, in a society such as ours, sustained distinction requires a sustained commitment to change.

At any historical moment, a great deal about society's views can be learned from that society's particular array of institutions of higher education and their programs. By observing admission and enrollment decisions we can learn who society believes should receive the most advanced education. By observing the educational and scholarly commitments we can learn something of the importance of traditional values, the weight attached to innovation, the most vital sources of knowledge and wisdom, the value placed on particular cognitive abilities, the most highly prized virtues, and the nature of the broad hopes and aspirations of the society itself.

Typically, in a liberal democracy different groups in society have quite diverse educational objectives. These different objectives are a critical reflection of our pluralistic and rapidly changing community, but our society cannot support a range of institutions as wide as our varied preferences. Conflicts between satisfying individual needs and the fulfillment of social obligations are inevitable. A liberal society is always in the process of locating the precarious balance between protecting individual freedom and ensuring sufficient solidarity. Even a liberal society cannot accommodate the entire spectrum of diverse beliefs because almost every right involves a claim against others. Therefore, it is hardly surprising that there is ongoing controversy regarding the appropriate shape of the curricula and scholarly commitments of the institutions of higher education. Nor is it astonishing that these controversies are most heated in societies, such as ours, characterized by rapid change and a rapidly accumulating knowledge base, in which higher education has become almost a requirement to be eligible for a full set of opportunities.

Given the current pace of change and the complex contemporary mission of the American research university, certain continuing pressures on these institutions are inevitable, including the tensions between and among:

1. Current circumstances and aspirations
2. The university's role as educator (requiring closeness and responsiveness to society) and critic (requiring distance from and skepticism of the status quo)
3. Specialization and integration
4. The demands for scholarship, the demands for education, and the demands for other services the university provides
5. Demands for diversity and independence vis-à-vis rising demands for social solidarity, responsiveness, and community.

The "right" profile of any university will vary by institution and geography, but in all cases will remain elusive and controversial. In a sector as heterogeneous as contemporary U.S. higher education, the idea of civic purposes must be understood as requiring different responses from differently situated institutions. However, none of these institutions should be misconstrued as institutions designed to preserve a portfolio of special entitlements granted to students, teachers, and scholars, yet withheld from other citizens. The special freedoms and privileges enjoyed by university communities, whether public or private, must be seen as mechanisms to enable universities to meet their responsibilities more effectively and more equitably. The intellectual and educational autonomy granted the university and the privilege of tenure are hardly ancient rights or rites, but rather instruments through which the university can more effectively pursue its public purpose. Tenure, for example, is an instrument to protect the faculty from inappropriate interference with the freedom to pursue their intellectual and educational agenda. Correspondingly, it is the faculty's responsibility to use this freedom to critically reexamine our current set of beliefs and commitments in their areas of expertise. Lapses in fulfilling this responsibility undermine the future of this idea more, in my judgment, than the occasional misinformed critique of tenure as simple job security. The intellectual and educational autonomy of the university and the faculty should be viewed in a similar fashion, not as an ancient right that must be defended but rather in terms of its current public purpose. That is, in what way does the autonomy of universities and their faculty serve and promote the underlying civic responsibilities of higher education? There are compelling reasons for society to continue to support these so-called privileges, but they are seldom publicly articulated.

Moreover, in the evolving world environment, the civic functions or public purposes of universities are perceived by many to have crossed national boundaries. Many universities, therefore, have become increasingly international institutions, especially as regards their student bodies, their faculty, and their research programs. For good or ill, however, their support base has remained much more local. It is the responsibility of the university community to exert the moral and intellectual energy necessary to convince its local supporters that this transformation serves everyone's interests. Indeed, I believe that the growing interdependency between the American research university and its counterparts abroad provides a useful model for other American institutions in an emerging world environment in which economic, intellectual, and cultural leadership will be much more widely and uniformly distributed across the globe.

As one imagines the future of the American university, it is quite clear that its functions and responsibilities will once again be transformed, at least partially, by new advances in science and technology, by our changing understanding of the human condition, by changing perspectives on how to live a meaningful life, by new ideas regarding our responsibilities and relationships with societies elsewhere in the world, and by evolving social views regarding the importance and use of new knowledge and advanced training. The historical record makes clear that eventually no facet of higher education is exempt from the impact of social change. The institutional history of American higher education reflects at its very base the need for a continuing examination of the relationship between the polity and the educational institution. Unlike many of the great European universities, the first American colleges were established not by independent groups of faculty and students or by royal initiative, but by private and public communities, and they were meant to serve important civic purposes. This was, perhaps, the first of the distinctively American contributions to the social structure of higher education.

One key characteristic of the American research university that I believe must be retained whatever the changes that lie ahead is its dual role as both society's servant and society's critic. These universities must, therefore, continue to provide programs that the society itself has identified as important as well as raising those questions and issues that society does not want to address. In some ways, universities can meet their responsibilities only by being a nuisance to the existing order of things. Given that for the research university there are no uncontested ideas, it may well be inevitable that it will continue to exist in an unresolved state of anxiety with the status quo. The university will need to continue to provide those programs demanded by the society that supports it, while resisting the temptation to simply mold the younger generation in the image of its elders. Inherent in such a concept is the belief that the future is a carrier of new possibilities for humankind.

RETAINING OUR SPECIAL ROLE: THE CHALLENGE OF
NEW PARTNERS, NEW SPONSORS, NEW ARRANGEMENTS,
AND COMMERCIALIZATION

One of the more serious issues many universities now face is the growing sway of private for-profit entities in the worlds of education and scholarship. Perhaps the most notable sources of this influence in recent years have come from the increase in joint ventures between universities and for-profit enterprises in engineering, biomedical research, and, increasingly, teaching. These alliances have also been facilitated by institutional developments and/or speculative environments in capital markets of the 1990s that allowed early-stage ideas to be transformed into hard cash rather quickly. Finally, there is the cautionary tale of "big time" intercollegiate athletics, which has become a thoroughly integrated component of the nation's commercial entertainment business. Indeed, in certain areas we in higher education are experiencing an almost relentless growth in the commercialization of education and scholarship.

This development has many interrelated causes. In part it is a result of the growth of for-profit institutions of higher education that have found educational niches that do not require direct subsidization, although their students are often dependent on the availability of federal and state financial aid. In part it is a result of developments on the scientific frontier and in financial markets that are changing the balance of forces between for-profit and not-for-profit research enterprises. In the last two decades, for example, industry's sponsorship of the nation's research and development has grown from a share of less than half to more than two-thirds. Within the university, the share of research sponsored by corporations has almost doubled during this same period. This increase is partly a result of explicit public policies aimed at the elimination of barriers between academic and industrial research, and partly a result of the increasing commercialization of intellectual property. In the period 1995–2000, industrial expenditures on research and development grew almost threefold while university expenditures for research and development grew by only one-third! This commercialization is creating both new opportunities and new barriers to free and open communication among members of the scientific community. Substantial disagreement remains as to where, as a matter of principle or social utility, to lodge the ownership of new ideas. Does it belong more with society at large or with individual proprietors? The resolution of this matter depends in part on whether or not the private ownership of new ideas, in either copyright or patent form, is defined as a temporary or quasi-permanent privilege. Finally, the greater presence of for-profit enterprises within the academy results from the never-ending quest of both faculty and administrators, acting in isolation from each other and from colleagues at other universities, to multiply the resources at their disposal.

For any university acting alone it is a relatively straightforward matter to define expected costs and benefits. Such calculations ignore, however, the costs for higher education as whole. Moreover, it is easier for the university acting alone to identify the benefits of increasing its involvement with private markets— which are mainly internal and accrue in the short run—than to identify the costs, which are more difficult to assess, lie further in the future, and are more likely to fall on the shoulders of the community of research universities as a whole rather than on individual institutions. This is especially the case in a radically decentralized higher education system such as ours. As a result, important collective goods that are central to the ability of the academic community as a whole to meet its responsibilities to the worlds of education and scholarship could be compromised or lost. There is nothing wrong in principle with joint efforts between universities and for-profit enterprises. Indeed, substantial societal benefits may result from such cooperation. Nonetheless, however, seductive these activities may be, we must examine them carefully, because although the short-term costs are minimal, the possible long-term costs are easy to overlook.

For good or ill, the increased presence of for-profit entities in education and research has altered the incentive structures in an arena where until recently universities had been enjoying a quasi monopoly of sorts. Of course new ideas have always come from a variety of sources and there have always been a variety of venues for advanced training. The problems with these new arrangements however, go beyond the natural controversy about the just distribution of costs and benefits between partners in a joint venture. There are reasons why for-profit and not-for-profit institutions were set up under different arrangements: either because their social roles were different or because the incentives of private markets were not thought to be appropriate to the public purpose of certain entities. Simply put, not all activities

17

and relationships in our society are appropriately situated in the commercial realm. I am particularly concerned with the impact of these joint ventures on the roles of the university as an independent source of knowledge and as a thoughtful critic of society. In the biomedical sciences, for example, it is very difficult to find disinterested researchers to evaluate new research. In short, society may not always be well served by merging the interests and priorities of the university with those of for-profit enterprises. Markets may maximize output and provide unparalleled efficiency and they may help preserve the "natural" rights to private property and freedom from coercion, but they cannot provide for important public goods and may, in fact, generate ethically unacceptable outcomes.

At the same time, it may be healthy to remind ourselves that in the early 1950s, many within the university community worried whether their increasing dependence on the federal government, especially in the area of research, would threaten the intellectual and educational independence of universities and faculty. This joint venture is now about fifty years old, and most observers believe that it has been beneficial to both parties. Perhaps the independence of universities has been somewhat protected by the competitive, open peer-review system under which federal sponsorship of research is allocated in the United States. Some critics of this system maintain that those already at the federal trough are setting the rules for the benefit of the current generation of "established" investigators and institutions. There is some truth to this, but it also provides the country with much greater assurance both that government resources are being well used and that the independence of universities is at least somewhat protected.

Biomedical Research

Consider first the growing influence of private for-profit activities in the arena of biomedical research. As the twenty-first century begins to unfold, both the nature and context of biomedical science are changing dramatically. In part the nature of biomedical science is being transformed by the imperatives arising on the scientific frontier. In addition, the context of the biomedical sciences is being reshaped by changes in the structure of those institutions that sponsor and/or nurture the entire enterprise. The resulting structure of opportunities and incentives facing biomedical scientists has the potential to change the relationships among the communities of biomedical investigators in academia, industry, and government, as well as between investigators and the institutions nurturing their work.

On the scientific frontier, a great deal of cutting-edge work now requires, for example, more expensive instruments and highly specialized facilities, high-throughput technologies and the assembling of large interdisciplinary teams. The availability of sequence databases, for example, is revolutionizing the manner in which the structure and function of bio-molecules are studied. Large databases and biological repositories and the associated software tools have become essential resources for investigators. As a result biocomputing and bioinformatics infrastructures have become indispensable tools for processing vast amounts of data as well as for modeling biological processes.

It seems clear from these few examples that the nature of scientific developments on the biomedical frontier requires new approaches as well as new institutional arrangements. Perhaps responsibilities within the biomedical enterprise should be distributed differently among the key actors—universities, academic health centers, pharmaceutical companies, government laboratories and agencies, federal sponsors, and nonprofit research groups. For example, should projects involving the use of high-throughput technologies be left to industry? Perhaps the current disciplinary organization of the biomedical sciences should be abandoned. I have some sympathy for the idea that developments across the scientific frontier require the reorientation of a good deal of science and science education. Nowadays more and more scientists need to feel at home with biology, mathematics, and computation as well as the physical sciences. Moreover, substantial aspects of our research efforts in biology now require cooperation and participation as well with the so-

19

cial sciences and even philosophy. Contemporary developments in genetics, after all, may not only change our understanding of the notions of human identity, human equality, and human freedom, but cause us to rethink the standards and norms through which we organize our society. All these matters certainly need to be informed by science, but must also be informed by resources from other areas of human understanding.

It is claimed by some that the rapidly increased sponsorship of research by for-profit companies at the nation's academic health centers threatens to undermine the faculty's academic freedom in biomedical science. Some suggest that the research agenda of the university faculty has become dominated by purely commercial considerations as opposed to intellectual values and the public good. Whether the public welfare is best served by a research agenda shaped by contemporary market forces or by the scholarly priorities of a relatively independent professoriate is an open issue. I am convinced that there are social benefits to a mixed strategy that retains a role for both. Although I find quite astonishing the degree to which university faculty have protected the academic interests of their institutions and colleagues, it is difficult to find any faculty member in the biomedical sciences who does not have a link to a for-profit entity, either as a recipient of research funds or as a consultant regarding the development of new products. Moreover, the Bayh-Dole Act of 1980, which allows universities to patent inventions that were financed by funds from governmental sources such as the National Institutes of Health, has catapulted universities and segments of their faculty deeply into the commercial sector, changing the very nature and extent of university-industry relations. Although the impact of these factors can be exaggerated, it is clear that academic medicine, for example, is no longer as autonomous as it once was. Academia's relationship with for-profit enterprises now extends well beyond the individual scientific investigator to include a large cohort of important university decision makers, including presidents and trustees. Nevertheless, there are few rules, regulations, or well-established precedents to provide appropriate oversight to the inevitable financial conflicts of interest for both institutions and institutional decision makers.

The question remains: Are these changes, on balance, a good or a bad thing? From one perspective, this increase in collaboration is a good thing in that it more fully integrates the nation's biomedical and other resources in a joint effort to combat disease and otherwise improve the human condition. From another perspective, it creates a virtual flood of conflicts of interest within academic institutions, where it becomes less and less clear whose interests are being served by the collaboration. Certainly, the new alliance undermines traditional notions of faculty and university independence, the full participation of faculty in the intellectual commons, and the role of university faculty as disinterested creators and arbiters of knowledge. It may ultimately undermine the reputation of universities for independence and openness and eventually reduce public trust in the entire university enterprise. Indeed, as more and more scientists occupy roles in both academia and industry, the public, increasingly concerned about possible sources of bias in "expert" opinion, has become less certain where to turn for truly disinterested opinions.

There can be little doubt that the increasing number of alliances between faculty and universities and various commercial entities, particularly pharmaceutical companies and biotechnology ventures, supported by venture capital has accelerated the transfer of scientific discoveries into practice. As a result, the flow of money to investigators and universities has increased, creating incentives for ever more vigorous pursuit of intellectual property rights. Understandably, this has increased the desire of many faculty and their universities to increase the likelihood of financial gain from their participation in the biomedical arena. Reinforcing these trends is the diminishing capacity of academic health centers to finance their own faculty's research.

One result of all this is an incentive for university-based investigators to make overly optimistic claims about real and potential discoveries. Another, more important one is the refusal of faculty to share material with colleagues, the sale of licenses becoming the primary vehicle to share knowledge. The biomedical enterprise, in other words, is undergoing a general retreat from the very idea of the commons of the mind, which for decades had defined both it and the university. This retreat has become serious enough to provide a number of serious academic based efforts to reopen the scientific literature and promote the greater sharing of intellectual and other scientific resources. For example, the Public Library of Science is a recently formed nonprofit organization of scientists now publishing its own journals and committed to making new scientific ideas, methods, results, and conclusions freely available to the public. There is widespread recognition that the vitality of the scientific enterprise requires access to the evolving knowledge base. Indeed, in 1992 the International Network for the Availability of Publication was formed to support such access on an international basis. Other forces, however, continue to pull in the opposite direction. In the public policy arena, for example, the U.S. government is using legislation and trade agreements to strengthen patent and copyright protection even further.

In summary, the extraordinarily rapid growth in science and technology, together with the closing temporal distance between certain traditional academic activities and commercial opportunities, has placed some strain on existing mores and practices in higher education, perhaps undermining the university's role as society's independent critic and arbiter. Given the character of current research practices, the necessity of disentangling individual versus community claims to intellectual property has become ever more pressing.

Although issues surrounding claims to intellectual property within a university context remain contested, I believe that the development of intellectual property is best thought of as the joint effort of many members of the university community and beyond, as well as the university itself, which has usually invested considerable resources in the matter. We often forget that even the idea of personal property is historically and culturally contingent, and may or may not be just. Our notions of personal property, of what we consider private, and of what we consider public matters are not culturally or economically neutral. Similarly, the notion that ideas can be appropriated as private intellectual property is also historically and socially contingent. As with personal property, it may be either a productive or an unproductive social concept. A good deal depends on our objectives. My own view is that the development of new knowledge is for the most part a collective social enterprise and we should use caution in assigning personal property rights in this arena. In any case, as with all new ideas developed as joint projects, it remains difficult to assign relative weights to the various property claims. Still, reasonable solutions should be available if we can keep our attention focused on the needs of the academic community and society as a whole.

We should understand that these basic problems arise because the teaching and research activities of the faculty are now perceived to have substantial monetary value to interests outside the university. This value raises the question not only of the equitable allocation of potential revenues, but also of the legitimate stake of the university and members of the university community in the allegiance of the faculty to the institution. The university has a legitimate obligation to protect the intellectual capital of the community against expropriation by institutions or individuals who seek a free ride on the work and resources of the entire community.

In an earlier time, when revenue streams, if any, were more speculative or relatively abstract concepts, there seemed little point in worrying about these matters. Indeed, in more innocent times these incentives were often thought to help support the university's overall mission. Today, however, no financial incentive exists to induce any party to rebalance the status quo. Meanwhile, there are too few leaders in positions within the faculty or administration pushing to revitalize the university's most important academic values. On a less sobering note, what now threatens to happen within academic science has already happened in intercollegiate athletics. Here, commercial interests have become dominant and no one has any financial incentive to change the situation; meanwhile, few seem to place enough value on the accumulating dangers to the university's most distinctive social functions to call for some change. I will return to this issue later in this essay.

Teaching

A somewhat analogous situation has arisen in the arena of teaching. Developments in computing and information technologies, which are beginning to enrich pedagogy on campus in important ways, also offer the prospect that campus-based faculty can effectively teach others "at a distance." To the extent that these latter activities proceed under the sponsorship of external organizations, a number of thorny issues may arise regarding the ownership of the intellectual property involved, the use of the university's name, quality control, conflicts of interest and/or commitment, and the accommodation of competing claims to any revenue streams involved.

The nation's faculties have built up an enormous store of materials and ideas that provide the overall structure and content of their courses. Given the new technological capacity to convert this capital into instructional programs to be delivered over the Internet, private interests have mobilized the financial capital needed to capture a new revenue stream from students unable to study on campus. This reformation is in some ways similar to the new horizons opened to the nation's recording companies when a new technology made it possible and profitable to convert their accumulated library of recordings into the new compact disk format. A closer analogy, using an old technology that also provides a format for teaching "at a distance," is the writing of textbooks by faculty. In this latter case, long-established traditions treat the intellectual property involved as belonging exclusively to the faculty member involved. This arrangement has worked well, although it has always been understood that the intellectual property incorporated in the textbook was at least partly a social product that included many contributions from colleagues and students as well.

The new technology supporting the Internet and the new possibilities it creates for "teaching at a distance" are sufficiently radical that many believe it useful to revisit existing traditions regarding the ownership of the intellectual property involved. The particular question arises: Who owns the accumulated instructional capital now ready to be converted into a radically new format?

Typically, two sets of university policies are involved in this issue. First is the set of policies that speak to conflicts of interest and conflicts of commitment. Second is the set of policies that deal with copyright and patents. Copyright and patent policies of universities are not completely coherent or consistent because they have been shaped by "historic rights" of quite different sorts. I have already outlined the policy with respect to textbooks. The policy with respect to patents has quite a different form, because historically universities have claimed ownership of this form of intellectual property. The property claim with respect to patents stems from the university's role as the legal entity that receives funds from external sources and serves as a kind of trustee on behalf of both sponsor and researcher particularly in the area of scientific and engineering research. Thus we live with two polar solutions: In the case of books and other copyrightable materials, the individual faculty are granted ownership of the intellectual property, whereas in the case of patents, ownership is presumed to fall to the university itself. Given these remarkably different approaches plus the ambiguity concerning whether software is copyrightable or patentable, it is clear that university policies regarding copyright and patent as well as conflict of commitment/interest may now need clarification, reinterpretation, and/or modification.

For example, existing policies that limit the amount of teaching faculty can do outside the university need to be clarified in relation to "distance or Internet learning." Also, do these policies apply to teaching outside the academic year? As with all new situations, I believe we should approach these and associated questions in a flexible manner; although we may not yet fully understand the issues, we should not be paralyzed while awaiting fuller understanding. For example, it may be useful to ask ourselves which of these nontraditional faculty teaching activities require mere disclosure to departmental leadership and which require a more formal agreement between the university and the faculty member involved. Similarly, we need to clarify how to apply the university's copyright and patent policies to "distance teaching," especially when such programs require some ongoing interaction with faculty and/or students, or to "courseware" more generally. In addition, we may need to broaden our definition of teaching if we are to be confident that these new activities support rather than undermine the university's core mission.

Regardless of the technology used, the mere fact that a university faculty member teaches elsewhere potentially undermines demand for the institution's campus-based offerings. Perhaps the key dividing line with such "conflicts of commitment" is whether faculty interaction and feedback is required to carry the instruction forward. With respect to copyright ownership of the materials, perhaps the key distinction is whether the university has made a specific additional commitment of resources to that particular project. When it has not, ownership of copyright would remain with the faculty member(s). In either case, appropriate recognition of the joint nature of the product should be recognized by some type of formal agreement and/or policy. Meanwhile, the university should remember that asserting even partial ownership claims over materials such as books, in which the faculty has enjoyed certain "historic rights," is much more difficult than asserting copyright claims where new technologies are involved.

To summarize: In the area of copyright material, one could assume faculty ownership whereas in the area of patents, one could assume university ownership—except for unusual circum-

26

stances in either case. Such circumstances would include situations where substantial additional university resources have been invested in the project; special university-owned collections have been used; the university's name is being used to promote the distribution of the product; or the university's approval is implied. (The university should probably require both disclosure and permission for the use of its name in any form.) To me, the key objective is to find some way to locate the mutually beneficial arrangements between faculty and university that promote their interests in tandem. Any policy ought to include a dispute resolution mechanism that involves representatives of the faculty.

Further confusing the issue is the current ambiguity of the nation's patent and copyright laws regarding intellectual property in diverse areas such as text, software, algorithms, and/or DNA molecules. It is not yet clear whether our current patent system can adapt successfully to the new technologies being developed, distinguish between the claims of novelty and utility and their reality, provide appropriate incentives for the growing service sector, insure the dissemination of knowledge, and achieve a level of harmonization with the patent systems that govern our trading partners. The extraordinary pace of innovation at both the laboratory and institutional level certainly raises serious concerns. Patents are more eagerly sought and defended than ever, even though they are more expensive to acquire and protect against infringement. In fact, there is great uncertainty regarding the ultimate impact of our traditional patent system outside traditional areas such as manufacturing and agricultural chemicals. Moreover there is great uncertainty about what kinds of innovation might be eligible for patent protection and the increasing costs of patent litigation. Taken together, these costs and uncertainties could discourage innovation and investment. Indeed, economic theory is ambivalent about the impact of the patent system on innovation and overall economic welfare. My main point, however, is that the drive by faculty and their universities to gain the fullest economic benefits of any discovery within a university setting even though they are already heavily subsidized greatly complicates existing relationship by generating serious conflicts of interest. This is one more area where the actions of a single university or group of universities can have important effects on other institutions. Some novel ideas to deal with these new factors are urgently required.

Intercollegiate Athletics

In terms of revenue and expenditure, "big time" intercollegiate athletics is getting bigger and bigger. Overall, however, there are many more financial losers than winners among intercollegiate athletic programs. Too many university presidents and their boards overestimate the probability that their programs will be financially successful. Moreover, the evidence suggests that even successful programs generate little in the way of increasing philanthropy or improving the university's ability to attract better students. Increased revenues and expenditures can be traced primarily to the increased commercialization of intercollegiate athletics. Although "big time" intercollegiate athletics has become a major commercial activity relatively recently, it has been a source of angst within the academic community for many years.

The appropriate role of athletics in higher education depends on a variety of cultural factors that derive not only from one's view of athletics, but from one's view of the role and function of universities. There are, therefore, a variety of views regarding the place of athletics in institutions of higher education. For some, athletics is, at most, just another extracurricular activity no different than the glee club or student newspaper. For them, intercollegiate or intramural athletic programs are appropriate parts of the university community but hardly deserving of the resources devoted to them and certainly not with the risks involved in allowing them to become integrated with the nation's commercial entertainment business. To others, athletics is one of the performing arts, perhaps like dance, opera, or musical performances. For them, it actually has a certain academic value delivered to the mind, and body. As such it should be supported (i.e., subsidized) in the same manner as other academic programs, and should aim for distinction but need have no connection to the nation's commercial entertainment network. For still others, athletics may be seen as professional training intimately tied to the demands of professional athletes. In this case, however, it is not at all clear why it should be part of higher education. Indeed, none of these approaches require tying intercollegiate athletics to the commercial entertainment business, and because it is always a challenge to accommodate both commercial and academic interests, it remains a puzzle how the current structure arose. The explanation, I believe, lies in the university's inexhaustible demand for resources and the desire of university leadership to be regarded as a successful participant in an important American enthusiasm.

In truth, why should an institution whose primary devotion to education and scholarship devote so much effort to competitive athletics? To many, the cultural process that led to this result is a mystery. To others, sport and physical fitness have had an association since the time of Plato's academy (which was located next to the gymnasium). Indeed, the ancient Greek notion that physical fitness supported intellectual acuity and even moral fitness still has resonance. Yet such Greek ideals were absent from the minds and hearts of the founders of both the medieval universities and the Colonial universities of America. The extent to which intercollegiate athletics has become such a prominent aspect of American universities' public image and the unusual devotion of so many of its students, staff, alumni, citizens, and even faculty are distinctive and new. Many in the American academic community believe that intercollegiate athletics, however valuable for both participants and spectators, exists on the margins of university life. Yet no other university activity takes up as much printed space in the daily newspapers, occupies as much verbal space in conversations of alumni, state legislatures, and citizens, or inspires such widespread fervor. Competitive sports are popular everywhere, but only in America are they so closely associated with universities.

So what, many may note, if intercollegiate athletics takes the lion's share of space in the popular media? They take up a small part of the budgets and staffs of most universities, and the core missions of American higher education have prospered; indeed, many believe that the United States has developed the best system of higher education in the world. Indeed, it is my strong impression that although most of my presidential colleagues are acutely aware of the problems in intercollegiate athletics, they also perceive that the cost of dealing with both external and internal constituencies on these matters is not worth the benefit. Better by far to focus on improving the university's education and research programs. Other observers from the academic community, however, feel that even relatively small activities that undermine the integrity or basic values of an institution represent a threat to its social legitimacy. A little history may help clarify some of these issues.

Intercollegiate athletics was not always such an integral part of American higher education. Indeed, in the Colonial college, organized competitive athletics was actively frowned on, and the first intercollegiate games were student-sponsored events often played in quasi-secret locations. The growing prominence of intercollegiate athletics is a twentieth-century phenomena. It coincided with the gradual transformation of the antebellum college into the more secular, vastly expanded institutions of American higher education that we know today. Leaders of American higher education in the early years of the twentieth century were probably as astonished at the drawing power of competitive sports and its grasp on the imagination of their constituencies as they were of the rapid secularization of their institutions. In any case, they soon became addicted to it. For decades, colleges and universities have systematically expanded their commitment to intercollegiate athletics. In the process, they have formed groups such as the various athletic conferences and the National Collegiate Athletic Association (NCAA) to regulate competition and to award memberships in particular coalitions. Although such self-regulation may be quite sensible, the perceived value of winning has always provided an incentive to explore how the agreed-on rules of engagement could be "bent." In retrospect, it seems clear that whatever the source of the incentive to "bend" the rules or otherwise behave hypocritically, universities have shown an almost relentless determination to do so and the cumulative effect has undoubtedly damaged their integrity.

Some consider the development of intercollegiate athletics, whatever its other problems and/or dividends, a successful strategy of responding to a major American passion in order to gain public support for colleges and universities that they must otherwise forgo. If this particular dividend allows us to pursue our primary objectives in education and scholarship, should we not perhaps overlook the inconveniences relating to our integrity? In the years that I was president of the University of Michigan, I traveled around the state a great deal. Everywhere I went, I found children playing in schoolyards wearing University of Michigan jerseys; often they imagined themselves representing the University of Michigan at some crucial juncture in a key athletic contest. The same was true of teenagers and many adults. This identification through sports was perhaps the only way for the University to remain part of the daily imagination of alumni as well as a wide spectrum of citizens of the state of Michigan. I vividly recall several trips to Pasadena when Michigan was playing in the Rose Bowl. In the evening preceding the game, a pep rally would be held in one of the large ballrooms in Los Angeles. The highlight of the evening was the truly talented 250-person Michigan marching band playing, at full volume, endless repetitions of the Michigan fight song while five thousand sophisticated alumni from every walk of life pleaded with them not to stop! Somehow Nobel prizes do not elicit such animation . . . although I hope they elicit even greater admiration.

When I became president of Princeton, one of my first surprises was the amount of alumni mail I received from Princeton alumni on the subject of intercollegiate athletics. I had assumed, quite naively, that intercollegiate athletics in the Ivy League would have a lower profile. Nothing could have been farther from the truth, although the issues were quite different from those I had encountered in the Big Ten. Indeed, it quickly became apparent that in some ways intercollegiate athletics was much more important at Princeton than at Michigan! On reflection, the reasons were simple. Princeton fielded many more teams than Michigan did, with an undergraduate student body about one-sixth the size. As a result, the number both of athletes recruited and of students participating in intercollegiate athletics formed a much higher proportion of the student body than at Michigan, and the proportion of Princeton alumni who had participated in intercollegiate athletics was also much larger than that of Michigan alumni. The proportion of participating students is critically important, because its relative size determines its potential impact on the institution's academic program. For institutions such as Princeton, sustaining the quality of their academic program places considerably more constraints on the academic profile of recruited intercollegiate athletes and, therefore, on the possibility of being competitive at the national level, because usually there is a negative correlation between athletic ability/motivation/talent and its academic equivalent.

Organized and competitive college athletics unquestionably benefits many young men and women and other members of the broader community. Enthusiasts claim that participation in intercollegiate sports can build admirable qualities of character such as self-sacrifice, discipline, focus, and the capacity to work with others toward a common objective. I have no doubt that this is often the case, although such traits can also be achieved in intramural sports, alternative athletic pursuits, and many other activities that require dedication, teamwork, and hard work. Moreover, competitive athletes may also cultivate other less admirable traits such as the determination to win at any cost (including the use of banned substances to enhance performance), and a rejection of the university's core academic values. In fact, I believe there are unavoidable tensions between the commercial

32

for-profit entertainment world of which "big time" intercollegiate athletics has become an integral part and an academic world that takes seriously its role to provide independent intellectual and moral leadership.

An ample and growing body of evidence indicates that this tension has already led many universities not only to adopt hypocritical attitudes and double standards in dealing with different members of their community, but to tolerate, over considerable periods of time, a good deal of antisocial and immoral behavior. Students are quite expert at understanding the difference between what we profess and what we do. The moral lessons we teach on our campuses come from actions, not propaganda. Athletics gets a good deal of public attention, but so do the many ethical lapses of students, coaches, administrators, university trustees, and occasionally faculty as they relate to the university's athletic programs.

The fact is that it may be impossible to be competitive in the athletic/entertainment business and also to stay true to the stated rules and principles of intercollegiate athletics. Commercial incentives in a "winner-take-all" marketplace not only may overwhelm the academic and moral integrity of the institutions involved, but also may involve the serious exploitation of some student athletes. Finally, as long as antitrust laws seem to prohibit the NCAA or other joint university efforts from regulating the commercial activities of its members, there may be no effective vehicle for reform. The Supreme Court has already opined that "big time" intercollegiate athletics is a commercial activity connected to the entertainment business. With almost sixty universities recording annual expenditures between twenty and sixty million dollars financed by university subsidies, ticket sales, television revenue, bowl game revenues, and various franchise arrangements, it certainly sounds like a commercial activity to me. Thus the very success of the enterprise as a commercial activity may eventually undermine the capacity of universities to place cooperative limits of any kind on the nature of the competition involved.

Despite the extraordinary growth in revenues generated by intercollegiate athletics, almost all universities and colleges must still subsidize their athletic programs. The vast majority of the increased revenues have gone to the expansion of intercollegiate program expenses stemming from the increased length of the season, increased travel budgets, increased salaries for coaches, increased athletic department staffs, and, in the last two decades, the expansion of the number of women's teams. Thus, although there is a great deal of rhetoric regarding the vast sums of money that intercollegiate athletics generates for the university, the facts are considerably more complex. It seems to me that if anyone is exploited in this process, it is probably the athletes in the so-called "big time" or revenue-generating sports, particularly football and men's basketball. Do these athletes receive what they deserve from the enterprise? I expect the answer would be different depending on the institution.

Although we may yet find a way to mitigate the worst aspects of the current system in "big time" intercollegiate athletics, it remains a cautionary tale regarding the difficulty of merging the interests of two different sectors of our society. Universities and for-profit organizations were set up under different arrangements for a reason, and merging them may or may not work. In any event, universities need to proceed cautiously with clear, nonnegotiable commitments to their most important values. In this area, as in many others, we must be clear about what we will not do, even for the money. My concern is that the rapidly increased commercialization of athletics at all levels may now pose a serious threat to the underlying integrity and independence of the university. It may also be a threat to itself, because there is also a growing danger that the long-cherished notion of an athletically gifted group of full-time students representing their alma mater in a high-spirited game will be revealed as illusory. If so, a separation may develop between the nation's elite athletes and higher education. An analogous separation between the best teenage athletes and the athletic programs of the nation's high schools is already well underway in many sports, a

development driven by the increasing commercialization, professionalization, and specialization of youth sports. In my view, it
is not possible to deal with the controversial issues in intercollegiate athletics without understanding the revolution that has
taken place in the way youth sports are organized in our country.
Because of this "revolution," athletes recruited for intercollegiate programs arrive on the nation's campuses with quite different notions of their purpose in attending university than was the
case a generation ago; universities themselves have quite different expectations, whether stated or unstated.

The separation of the nation's most gifted young athletes from
the athletic programs of academic institutions may or may not
be a useful development. On the one hand, lessening the association of academic institutions with the nation's most gifted young
athletes could serve the interests of both academic institutions
and the athletes themselves. Indeed, many athletes, their families, and various commercial interests have already taken this
path by pursuing their athletic goals outside the nation's intercollegiate programs. On the other hand, the nation's universities
are understandably loath to give up their connection to a popular American enthusiasm. It seems clear to me that it is becoming
harder and harder to distinguish intercollegiate athletics from
professional athletics. Increasingly coaches and players are being
recruited from a common pool, and intercollegiate athletics is
increasingly governed by the values and needs of the commercial
entertainment industry. Lessening universities' association with
"big time" athletics would have its costs and benefits, but it is
high time we started being more honest and realistic about the
costs of "big time" athletics to the academic community, because
the prospective benefits are easy to both enjoy and exaggerate.

Past history suggests that America's universities will opt for as
strong a continuing association with athletics as they can muster.
They will continue to pursue increased commercial revenues,
making the compromises needed to achieve this objective, with
a simultaneous if less focused effort to achieve certain "reforms"
that might limit the most serious compromises of academic val-

ues. Such reforms include attempts to limit practice times, increase revenue sharing between winners and losers, shift the structure of athletic scholarships, stiffen admissions requirements somewhat, and occasionally limit the expansion of season lengths in particular sports. Although such reforms are certainly useful, over time they will probably have a very limited impact and will be overwhelmed by the desire to win and to raise more revenue. Moreover, I would predict that both the cost of tickets and the level of institutional subsidy will increase substantially as efforts to contain costs prove ineffective.

My own view is that the only reforms that might enable the nation's universities to find a better balance among their business, educational, and political interests would be, first, to provide more genuine transparency so that everyone understands exactly what compromises have been made in the service of being "competitive"; second, to pursue more meaningful academic standards for *all* their students; third, to abandon the annual search for a national champion (see immediately below); and, finally, to find a more effective mechanism for collective action. The NCAA has performed and continues to perform many extremely valuable services for intercollegiate athletics, but as I have already noted, the courts now allow the NCAA rather limited authority to act on commercial matters and intercollegiate athletics is decidedly a commercial activity. Perhaps the existing structure could be "saved" if the NCAA received an exemption from antitrust regulation; this development appears quite unlikely. More likely is that an individual conference of like-minded schools would pursue new strategies. This would necessitate giving up on the idea of national champions that seems to underlie a good deal of the commercial revenues enjoyed by intercollegiate athletics. Nevertheless, I believe that if we restricted our aspirations to regional or conference-based championships, we might have many more happy fans, and even the media might have more fun trying to decide just who was best. In such an environment there might be six or eight teams who thought of themselves as national champions. I fail to see what harm would come from this. Failing such a proposal, which may strike many as naive, I return to the idea of greater transparency. At least that way, all constituencies can understand better the costs and benefits of the entire enterprise and either continue to support current trends or push for a realignment of values and aspirations. Social institutions have a complex array of privileges and responsibilities to the society that they serve and they are often required to compromise certain values in the pursuit of larger, but not purely self-serving objectives. Universities do this all the time as they search for a position of uneasy equipoise among the competing objectives that they wish to pursue. Perhaps intercollegiate athletics will remain an aspect of such a compromise.

CONCLUSION

In an environment that is changing, the university will inevitably be the subject of debates about the relationship of its existing programs' connectedness with its commitments to the changing needs of society. We must not avoid such discussions. In particular, we cannot view such an ongoing dialogue as undermining our traditional values and autonomy. Rather, it is through this dialogue that our most important traditional values, such as autonomy, can be reinforced. Indeed, autonomy implies a level of responsibility and thoughtful responsiveness that make such a dialogue imperative. Such a dialogue can also help reach a social consensus on the structure of the scholarly and educational agenda and the appropriate use of our ever-expanding knowledge base. In addition, such dialogues support the university's continuing role as both society's thoughtful but responsive servant and society's thoughtful but demanding critic.

In this regard it is also important to recall that any institution of education gains social legitimacy only by fulfilling the specific responsibility of providing the next generation with the capacities, beliefs, and commitments thought necessary to ensure soci-

37

ety's goals. The nature of the particular array of institutions of higher education that society supports at any moment reveals a great deal about that society's views. Simply put, the set of educational arrangements put in place at any moment is directly related to the nature of the society we wish to sustain or to the agreements we citizens have made about how we ought to relate to each other and what we value about the individual and his/her work. For example, the nature of undergraduate education for citizens of an emerging liberal democracy, with its increasing focus on individual autonomy and the inherent rights of all people to self-determination and its associated desire to find new and better arrangements in both science and society, must be quite distinct from the analogous set of arrangements in societies that have quite different political, cultural, and social objectives. Little wonder, therefore, that controversy—often socially productive controversy—usually surrounds these institutions.

In one critical respect universities must assume the leadership in the much-needed dialogue or conversation with other parts of society. In particular, it is up to the leadership of the research universities to sustain support for the notion that the research university cannot fully meet its responsibilities if its intellectual independence is lost or compromised. In my judgment university leaders can do so only by demonstrating that the nation's research universities are playing a significant role in moving society forward and that the universities' scholarly achievements are attentive to the innate human need to understand our place in the larger scheme of things. What gives human beings their distinctiveness is not simply their desire to know, understand, and give shape to their place and time on this planet, but also their complementary desire to give their efforts greater meaning. The university's intellectual independence comes with responsibilities not only to the world of scholarship, but also to the cultural and social aspirations we have for ourselves and our descendants.

For example, as American universities look ahead, there is no avoiding the fact that our society will continue to deal with the full implications of numerous forces such as globalization, the increasing interdependence of a wide array of institutions and their attachments to private market forces, and the constitutional status of group rights. In this context, universities will need to define their own role in enabling our increasingly interdependent and diverse societies to define themselves in constitutional, political, and socioeconomic terms. This will bring new responsibilities to the university both for the development of ideas (e.g., resolving the tension between the individual, various groups, and "the" community in a new context) and for understanding the curricular implications and scholarly imperatives of this new era. In our emerging environment, universities not only need a constantly refreshed vision of their role that reflects the emerging reality of their times, but also the intellectual energy to pursue their vision and to convince society to continue to envision them as an important component of society's own vitality. The distinguished university, like the biosphere, is in a constant state of evolution characterized by an ever-changing kaleidoscope of both opportunities and constraints. For the most distinguished of the nation's universities, the greatest challenge is not to fall victim to the dangers of entrenched success by failing to remember that no university is as distinguished as it says (or believes) it is, or as distinguished as it should be. Change may appear to be unnecessarily risky, but universities need to maintain a certain anxiety or uneasiness regarding whether or not their programs are continuing to meet their responsibilities in education and scholarship. Such anxieties and the honest self-examination they ought to occasion are essential ingredients in a university's capacity to build and maintain its excellence. In the decades ahead, anxiety, courage, energy, adaptation, leadership, and change are the price of continued distinction and relevance in higher education.

The Transformation
of the Antebellum College
FROM RIGHT THINKING TO LIBERAL LEARNING

IN THE DECADES since the Civil War, we have witnessed a radical transformation in the nature and size of American public and private institutions of higher education. Indeed, the nature and role of the antebellum college is, for most of us, a rather vague, unstable, and distant memory. The rather startling nature of the institutional transformation of the antebellum college is the primary subject of this essay. This bit of American higher education history has always held a certain fascination for me for two reasons. First, because the antebellum college seemed to provide such an unpromising foundation for meeting the emerging educational needs of America, its transformation into an energetic component of contemporary American life seemed a rather astonishing development. Second, I was intrigued by the puzzle of why the transformation of antebellum colleges, or their replacements, took so long to get under way. The transformation that eventually took place, of course, incorporated both a new set of institutional actors and a radically new set of social, educational, and scholarly commitments. To understand fully the belatedness of the change, as well as its character and speed, however, one needs to appreciate the nature of a broad set of initial conditions bequeathed by earlier developments, both at home and abroad. These initial conditions greatly influenced the character and dynamics of subsequent events. Indeed, any set of current institutional arrangements has a complex set of historical roots, and in the case of the contemporary American research university, the most popular narratives regarding its birth are too "thin."

The late nineteenth-century metamorphosis of American higher education may seem to be a well-worn topic whose broad outlines are familiar. Historical scholarship in this area, however, is modest in volume, and many issues remain outstanding. I do not intend to use this essay to merely restate the usual themes, but rather to focus on some elements of the social, political, and intellectual developments in Europe as well as in nineteenth-century America that are incompletely incorporated into our understanding of this important epoch.

For many scholars, the Civil War provides a convenient symbolic marker between two different eras in American higher education. Certainly, the intellectual vacuity of the early nineteenth-century American college inspired many observers to express the need for basic reforms throughout the first half of that century. Indeed, throughout the first half of the nineteenth century a small and scattered number of college presidents and individual faculty members were trying out and/or attempting to promote new approaches in an attempt to rescue the antebellum college from its academic irrelevance. By midcentury, Henry P. Tappan (1851, p. 52), the president of the University of Michigan, was promoting a new concept for America's universities as places where "provision is made for studying every branch of knowledge in full, for carrying forward all scientific investigations, where study may be extended without limit, where the mind may be cultivated according to its wants." Earlier, Thomas Jefferson had introduced a curriculum at the University of Virginia that offered much more choice to students, and in the early decades of the nineteenth century at Harvard, George Ticknor (1876) was promoting the notion that the curriculum had to be expanded. Others, such as Ralph Waldo Emerson and Francis Wayland (1842, 1850), attached themselves to a very popular sentiment of the time, namely, that we should find a distinctively "American way" in higher education just as we had in business and politics. At the same time, some reformers, such as Henry Tappan at the University of Michigan, worried that the commercial spirit of America might make the support of serious study difficult.

Although these worthy efforts did not take firm hold, it is important to remember that some of the seeds of the transformation of American higher education following the Civil War had been sown in the previous half-century. Indeed, the establishment of institutions such as the U.S. Military Academy at West Point and Rensselaer Polytechnic Institute (RPI) early in the nineteenth century, and the remarkably "modern" aspirations of the University of Pennsylvania, for example, foreshadowed the transformation that lay ahead for U.S. higher education, as did the rather isolated but occasionally distinguished efforts of particular faculty and/or departments. In this latter respect, we could hardly overestimate the importance of the work of luminaries such as Joseph Henry at Princeton University, J. Willard Gibbs at Yale University, and Louis Agassiz at Harvard University. Moreover, the justly celebrated Michelson-Morley experiments at the Case School of Applied Sciences took place very shortly after the Civil War and well before the eventual transformation of the Colonial colleges took place. Indeed, throughout the nineteenth century there were scattered attempts to broaden the curriculum, to separate religion from philosophy, to introduce aspects of the scientific method, and to undertake a number of scholarly initiatives. Nevertheless, these reforms did not take hold. Neither federal nor state governments interested themselves in promoting reform, and the antebellum college became a less and less relevant institution. The puzzle I wish to address is why the higher education sector was so "stuck" in the past while the society around it was eagerly incorporating change.

As in so many other areas of American life, the ending of the Civil War provided some of the momentum for the transformation of the antebellum college. In my view, the Civil War caused many to become increasingly skeptical about some of the cultural commitments of previous decades. People were ready not only for peace, but for an enriched, more pluralistic set of ideas to inform our national life. The national imagination was seized by the notion that a greater toleration of diverse views would lead to more satisfactory social, political, and cultural arrangements—even if many such views turned out to be in error. This concept was accompanied by a strong desire not to be driven again to civil carnage solely by differences in belief.

Interestingly, this new intellectual outlook was remarkably consistent both with some of the underlying principles of the emerging liberal outlook—the developing organization of private markets—and what I understand to be the notions behind Protestant universalism. Moreover, the political aftermath of the Civil War galvanized governments, both state and federal, to take increased responsibility for social and economic progress. This was reflected not only in higher education—with the establishment of the land grant colleges—but also in other areas, with the idea of national taxation, the completion of the transcontinental railway, and the first effective national currency.

Just as Europeans had to worry throughout the nineteenth century about the uncertainty, anxiety, and unpredictability of the modern world that was replacing the ancien régime, America in the post–Civil War era also had to find ways to accommodate new attitudes, incentives, and other social and cultural practices that would allow success in an increasingly industrialized society committed to liberal democracy and an economy organized around private markets. A society thus organized implied, among other things, a life of greater uncertainty and a more prevalent sense of loss. As wave after wave of social and economic innovation took hold, they inevitably brought in their wake a sense of loss for some and moral anxiety for all. Such turbulent moral seas characterized the society of an altered world as it worked out new rules regarding "just shares" and citizens' mutual obligations to each other.

In contrast to the dynamism generated by the waves of social, economic, and political change at the time, the tiny post–Colonial colleges that held sway in American higher education at least through the mid-nineteenth century seemed to be continuing to devote most of their energies to controlling unruly students and doing their best to instill a certain Christian piety and "right" thinking into their lives. The narrow academic curriculum focused on rote learning of classical languages and literature, rhetoric, some rather simple mathematics, and, of course, the "capstone" course in moral philosophy. The aim of the moral philosophy course was to show how the various bodies of knowledge, including both divinely revealed and empirical knowledge, related to each other and to a larger unity. The curriculum was firmly set within a Christian worldview that all knowledge, whatever its source, would reveal the truth of the scriptures. Perhaps these institutions might be thought of as a type of "sacred" place where the values and certain artifacts of a cherished past were to be protected from the contemporary developments that were taking society in different directions. In purely scholarly terms, it is perhaps best to think about these institutions as modest high schools in an era that preceded both mass and universal secondary education.

In general terms, erudition in pre–Civil War America flourished outside, not within, higher education. Little wonder, therefore, that few ambitious young people or their parents thought such a collegiate education very rewarding. Although the 1828 *Yale Report* declared that the purpose of collegiate training was "to lay the foundation of a superior education," this was hardly a reality at the time. In spite of the early voices pressing for change, and some early and rather novel experiments at places such as RPI and West Point, which were inspired, in part, by the development of France's *grandes écoles* and pressing national engineering tasks,[1] a sustained reform movement took hold only in the post–Civil War decades.

---

[1] The United States had a great need for technically trained military officers both for military purposes and for the related purpose of building canals and roads to knit the country together. This led to the establishment of the U.S. Military Academy at West Point in 1802, with the model of France's *école polytechnique* very much in mind (as opposed to the technical schools in Germany or the English apprenticeship system) and with the desire to graduate not merely engineers, but *officiers du génie*, so that officers would be men of science welcomed into the learned societies. In these early decades the actual curriculum, although similar in structure to the *école polytechnique*, did not reach nearly the levels of learning achieved in France. RPI, on the other hand, was founded in 1824 specifically for "the application of science to the common purposes of life," and at midcentury small "scientific schools" were begun at colleges such as Harvard, Yale, Dartmouth, and Michigan.

THE TRADITIONAL NARRATIVE

The traditional narrative surrounding the birth of the contemporary American university in the last decades of the nineteenth century often focuses on the impact of a few American academic tourists visiting German universities, who were inspired both by the "Humboldtian" vision of higher education that had begun to transform higher education in Germany and the wealth of scholarly resources available in Europe's great libraries.[2] More specifically and more fairly, the traditional narrative has not one, but three principal components. They are: (1) the influence of both new European ideals of scholarly inquiry, graduate education, and research (the "Humboldtian" vision) and the scholarly resources (e.g., libraries) needed to fulfill such a vision; (2) the impact of the founding and growth of new or reconstituted American institutions of higher education, especially the new public land-grant universities and new private institutions such as Johns Hopkins University, the Massachusetts Institute of Technology, the University of Chicago, the California Institute of Technology, and Stanford University; and (3) the implications of the refinement of scientific and scholarly procedures and the resulting increased importance of disciplinary specialization.

This narrative is accurate but incomplete. It needs to be complemented by a number of additional themes that were critical in shaping the revolution in American higher education. First, this traditional narrative needs to be enriched by a more thoughtful analysis of the reconstitution and expansion of both the arts and sciences as an academic curriculum and the arts and sciences faculty. Second, the evolving relationships among the arts and sciences, our new notions of a liberal education, and the increasingly specialized professional schools need to be incorporated. Third, we need a better understanding of the changing role of religious thought within American higher education and how matters of faith were accommodated within the new

---

[2] See, for example, Cohen 1998; Geiger 1986; Lucas 1994; and Ruch 2001.

social and cultural commitments of the university. Fourth, it is important to trace the continuing impact of the model of higher education provided by the British universities that were themselves being slowly transformed during this period. Finally, perhaps most important, the traditional narrative needs to be supplemented by a fuller understanding of the impact of a wide variety of economic, social, political, and intellectual developments that were transforming societies both here and abroad.

For example, we find no place in the traditional narrative to acknowledge the impact (or lack thereof) of the waves of intellectual development that were taking place in Europe during the eighteenth century, including the prevalent European sentiment that humankind was at the dawn of a new age of "oceanic globalization." Indeed, globalization had become a ubiquitous idea in late eighteenth-century Europe. More particularly, intellectual life had become transoceanic as the movement of goods, people, and ideas accelerated in all directions across the globe. This eighteenth-century European intellectual sentiment was similar to today's discussions about the increasing impact of new communication technologies on globalization. One of the questions that needs further investigation is why the intellectual life of the antebellum college turned its back on global sentiments such as this.

Moreover, European discontent with the monopoly of classical and biblical scholarship on the curricula of universities began in earnest in the seventeenth century and reached its maturity in Europe in the eighteenth century, when scholars and others began to doubt whether such exclusive dependence on this literature would serve the moral or political development of young people. Scholars from Michel Montaigne in the sixteenth century to Immanuel Kant in the eighteenth century were especially concerned that such a concentration, devoid as they believed it was of the imperatives of present-day contingencies, made students unable to become meaningful and wise actors in society's unfolding drama. Indeed, Kant favored more experimentation in education, even while acknowledging that some experiments would fail. Much earlier and from a very particular perspective, in the thirteenth century Roger Bacon had worried that the exclusive emphasis within university curricula on the classical languages and literatures had an unfortunate and malign influence on the development of science. In the seventeenth century, Francis Bacon (1861–74, p. 15) offered this direct but rather unfair observation: "The wisdom which we have derived principally from the Greeks is but like the boyhood of knowledge, and has the characteristic property of boys: it can talk, but it cannot generate; for it is fruitful of controversies, but barren of works." In a similar vein, John Locke (1899, p. 74) remarked, "what ado is made about a little Latin and Greek, how many tears are spent on it, and what a noise and business it makes to no purpose." Finally, Herbert Spencer (1900) had observed that instruction in Latin and Greek had little intrinsic value, but simply served the social function of separating "gentlemen" from less "worthy" persons. In any case, by the early nineteenth century, concern was widespread that the ancient universities and their ancient ways could be justifiably characterized as, in Thomas Macaulay's (1972, p. 17) phrase, "a glut of Greek, Latin, and Mathematics, and a lamentable scarcity of every thing else." By that time, many observers besides Spencer had come to question the unique capacity of the classical languages to train the mind or impart any special virtues. Within the walls of the antebellum college, however, there were few echoes of these views.

With respect to the antebellum college and its eventual successors, therefore, one aspect to the puzzle is to try to understand why the broad-based intellectual developments that were taking hold in Europe up to and throughout the eighteenth century took so long to be incorporated into the programs of American colleges. The theory that this had to await a few rather brief trips to Europe by certain college presidents or faculty seems less than fully satisfactory. Moreover, it does not explain the emergence of certain distinctive American characteristics that responded to the realities and aspirations of both American society and American higher education. For example, the distinctive American distrust of government and America's unusually strong faith in competition had a major impact on the nature and quality of the higher education sector that emerged. My own view is that although the competitive and decentralized system that emerged certainly has its excesses, on balance it has served both the nation's interests and the interests of the worlds of scholarship and education remarkably well.

In order to more fully explain the character of the transformation of the antebellum college, I will first turn my attention to the particular conditions present in both Europe and America in the nineteenth century because, as I have already noted, much of the traditional discourse surrounding the birth of the contemporary university pays insufficient attention to these contextual issues.

THE NINETEENTH-CENTURY CONTEXT: EUROPE

In Europe, the nineteenth century was a time of rapid population growth, urbanization, and a myriad of new challenges arising out of the social and economic disruptions occasioned by the industrial revolution, the French revolution, and new developments in communications and the natural sciences. The effects of the French Revolution and the continental wars that followed, as well as the rising social and cultural tensions between the new and the older elites that had been created by a significant reallocation of property, income, and status, were far-reaching indeed. The revolutions of the 1820s, 1830s, 1840s, 1850s, and 1871, which culminated in the abortive Russian revolution of 1905, are testimonies to the fact that European society was being transformed in a fundamental, revolutionary way.

The European nineteenth century can be defined intellectually as extending from John Dalton's atomic theory to Max Planck's quantum theory. It included a host of other astonishing intellectual developments that transformed our perception of human agency, how we experienced the natural world, our conception of the nature of human responsibility, and the structure of many social and political institutions. These developments included

Marxism, Charles Darwin's theory of evolution, Charles Lyell's work in geology, Louis Pasteur's work in microbiology, James Clerk Maxwell's theories of light, magnetism, and electricity, Auguste Comte's positivist philosophy, and Sigmund Freud's technique of psychoanalysis. Equally important was the transformation taking place in the humanities with entirely new approaches to the creation and study of literature and art. Most important in this latter respect was a vast expansion in the spectrum of cultural products—such as books, music, art, and art history—that were thought to shed light both on human aspirations and on the human condition. The desire that emerged to study these cultural products shared the same spirit that was animating scholarship in the natural sciences. Slowly, truth claims based on tradition, divine inspiration, and other subjective forms of knowing lost status in the intellectual environment of the newly constituted European universities. Inexorably, the idea took hold that purely empirical knowledge was preferable to philosophical and/or religious speculations. In this context there seemed less and less room for religious faith; for some, even ignorance seemed better than divine fiat.

Less fully appreciated about this same period is the remarkable increase in demand for information. In fact, the growth in population, production, and trade, along with the need to organize the rapidly growing knowledge base required by new forms of government and business stimulated its own nineteenth-century information revolution. New systems of classification, statistics, dictionaries, encyclopedias, and postal and telegraph systems were developed, new techniques in cartography arose, and with this came a dramatic increase in the movement of skilled workers across national borders. This revolution was far-reaching, affecting the manner in which information was gathered, stored, transformed, displayed, and communicated. Yet it has received less attention than the much more controversial intellectual and cultural issues of the era.

Perhaps this lack of attention is not surprising given that cultural issues were usually framed as a choice between science and reason, on the one hand, and religion and superstition, on the other; between tolerance and prejudice; between personal autonomy and the social contract; and between a new conception of justice and some form of continued absolutism. Yet the simple growth in intellectual thought, stimulated both by the rapidly increasing knowledge base and by new forms of information storage, transfer, and analysis, was as important an instrument of change as the revolutionary political and social movements of the time. Moreover, it was the nineteenth century that saw the idea take hold of revolution, or change, as a permanent condition, whether in the Marxian sense or in the liberal sense that new knowledge of the natural world would propel us to a permanent reevaluation of arrangements in science and society. This latter notion would have a great effect on the structure of higher education both in Europe and in America.

These stunning developments did not, of course, spring up on their own. Incidents in the previous century provided the platform on which new ideas in science and new societal arrangements of all kinds developed. Recall that the century between 1650 and 1750 was also the end of the European Middle Ages. This was the era, perhaps spurred by the great voyages of discovery, of revolutionary thinkers such as Isaac Newton, Gottfried Leibniz, Benedictus de Spinoza, Locke, David Hume, Robert Hooke, Denis Diderot, Daniel Bernoulli, Leonard Euler, and Voltaire, to name just a few. At last one could study the distant origins of modern science, the beginnings of the idea of progress, the first historical criticism of the Bible, and the true nature of the other great religions and cultures of the world. The last decades of the eighteenth century continued to witness great advances in our understanding of other cultures and of the natural world through the contributions of well-known figures such as Joseph-Louis Lagrange, Charles-Augustin de Coulomb, Humphrey Davy, William Herschel, Antoine-Laurent Lavoisier, and Joseph Priestly.

The eighteenth century was indeed an extraordinarily inquisitive age, but perhaps surprisingly a good deal of the new exploration of the natural world took place outside of the ancient European institutions of higher education. The universities were not central to the intellectual developments taking place. In fact in seventeenth- and eighteenth-century Europe, most genuine intellectuals regarded universities with complete disdain. Leibniz thought of them as monklike institutions that concerned themselves with sterile fancies. Adam Smith thought of them as the last refuge of discredited ideas. Although by the end of the eighteenth century a small number of universities such as those at Edinburgh, Göttingen, and Jena did house lively intellectual environments, these were exceptions.

In a partial response to a rapidly changing world, a number of German universities began early in the nineteenth century to remobilize themselves toward a more secular curriculum and to lay the foundation both for a new role for faculty and for university-based efforts in science and scholarship, including research training. This "new" German university is most closely associated with the figure of Wilhelm von Humboldt and the institution of the Humboldt University of Berlin. In Germany it was an age of romantic heroes, the age of Napoleon Bonaparte, Ludwig von Beethoven, Friedrich Schiller, and Johann Wolfgang von Goethe. Humboldt published a paper in 1789 that questioned religious dogmatism and defended freedom of intellectual inquiry, and through that paper he became the hero of the new German university. The basic ideas for the reformulation of the nature and the role of the university were not his alone, but he was the one who in a remarkably short period of time made the new Humboldt University of Berlin a reality by early in the nineteenth century.

The key characteristics of the new German university that were later to catch the attention of various American scholars and reformers were: preparatory studies should be left to the *Gymnasium*; teaching, research, and research training are a unified whole and must all be central to a university's social function; libraries must expand their scope; faculty must be granted academic freedom and independence; and the seminar should be developed as a focus for research and research training. As we shall see, each of these features would be adopted, if at all, in quite a different form in the American context.

The new emphasis on scholarship led to steadily increasing specialization and the resultant formation of a variety of new disciplines, especially in the social sciences and humanities. Moreover, the disciplines organized in the faculty of arts and sciences became the most important centers of scholarship rather than the professional schools such as law, medicine, and theology, which for many centuries had formed the heart and soul of the European university. Although the antebellum American college did not have strong faculties in the ancient learned professions, these European developments did affect the evolving structure of American higher education, which continued to put the disciplines of the arts and sciences at their core.

As the era of modernity dawned, European societies began to perceive themselves as entering a new and qualitatively different kind of period—an era that would at least allow universities to take on new responsibilities in the area of scholarship and research training; allow the traditional study of religion and the classics to be expanded and partially displaced by the reconstituted humanities, including "new" subjects such as history, literature, and art history; and enhance the legitimacy of secular and scientific learning. In a more general sense, the revival and transformation of higher education that began in Europe and reached America only somewhat later in the century followed a period of revival and growing faith in the primacy of reason and cognition, as well as faith in the potential of economic growth and technological and material progress to transform society for the better. Such objectives, however, would have to be earned in ways that required, among other things, the creation of new institutions and/or a transformation of existing ones. In France the leadership was taken by the new *grandes écoles*, while in Britain it was the Scottish universities that demonstrated a more progressive spirit. In America, as in France and Britain, it was the "newer" or the less elite universities rather than the older antebellum colleges that took the lead in redefining the social role of the university and the shape of its programs.

In Europe, particularly in Germany, France, and Britain, the sharpest controversies regarding university reform occurred during the first half of the nineteenth century, and the resulting changes in European higher education reflected, however belatedly, the enormous and profound shifts that were taking place in the economic, technological, social, political, and cultural bases of Western societies. The changes in European higher education at that time were perhaps among the last of the great liberal revolutions set in motion by the forces of the Enlightenment.

THE NINETEENTH-CENTURY CONTEXT: AMERICA

To me what remains most impressive about nineteenth-century America is that despite many unresolved social issues, especially the failure to extend the notion of individual rights to all citizens, and at least one major tragedy, the Civil War, America slowly put in place a portfolio of social, political, and economic mindsets that not only encouraged the development of new alternatives, but created a social capacity to implement new ideas and a willingness to replace, over time, large elements of the status quo. This required, among other things, a growing openness of the society and its ruling elites to new ideas developed here or elsewhere and embodied in products, persons, or ideas.

Particularly important in this respect was the development of political customs, practices, and traditions that on the one hand stressed local prerogatives, but on the other hand allowed members of Congress considerable authority over detailed matters that remained within their jurisdiction. In the U.S. system it was just as appropriate for Congress to control many of the administrative organizations and procedures of the federal government as its policies—that is to say, the means as well as the ends. These newly formed social and political traditions also reflected a deep distrust of the ruling establishment and political party in power, the religious establishment, and the role of experts, including faculty. It was the era of the "common man" and native American ingenuity. Such social and political norms more or less assured that no national plan for higher education would emerge.

These same traditions led to a rather distinct set of governance structures for American higher education, with less authority vested in the self-regulation of the faculty. America, with its almost traditional distrust of government (especially the federal government), its preference for ingenuity over scholarship, and its belief in competition, chose local instead of national governance (whether by the state or through a charter granted to a private group) and a relatively autonomous and decentralized system. Moreover, these same sentiments favored keeping control out of the hands of the local intelligentsia (i.e., the faculty or their representatives) and in the hands of community-based boards. As a result, the American university system now exhibits relatively greater differentiation (reflecting, in part, local conditions and priorities), less equality among schools, a more adaptive capacity (more opportunities for experimentation), and, in research-intensive institutions, a closer relationship between teaching and research than in their counterparts elsewhere (again reflecting the importance of community governance attached to education). These structural characteristics are, in my opinion, largely the result of the distinctively American social and cultural traditions discussed earlier.

These political and social customs were, for example, quite different than those being developed in Great Britain. In America, the struggle between the competing desires to hold government responsible, on the one hand, and to protect the freedom of action of the individual, on the other, was resolved in favor of the prerogatives and freedoms of individual and local government units. Indeed, the power of the president and Congress was severely restricted compared to the British prime minister and Parliament. Another example is that the U.S. courts are, in certain circumstances, able to restrain even the decisions of democratically elected legislatures. In Britain, however, the power of the courts is limited to the fair enforcement of whatever laws Parliament enacts.

More critical was the American attitude, developing as the nineteenth century progressed, of confidence in the future and faith in individual and local decisions. Of course, along with this growing self-confidence went a feeling of social dislocation among some as the processes of industrialization, urbanization, and immigration, unsettled established social norms and cultural institutions. Indeed, anxiety about the ultimate impact of modernity generated a wide selection of both utopian and dystopian novels, such as Mark Twain's *Connecticut Yankee in King Arthur's Court* (1889). Nevertheless, America came to embrace the notion that, despite these difficulties, the future was the carrier of new possibilities, and that private markets (somewhat shielded from foreign competition), the American version of a republican liberal democracy, new technology, and an expanding frontier would together launch America into a new era. Moreover, Americans as a whole were less concerned than Europeans about rapid change destroying the existing set of accumulated traditions and privileges. This developing national attitude was to prove vital for American higher education.

The American Economy

I turn next to an equally important set of nineteenth-century American conditions that related to the economy and the rapid growth of American wealth. If higher education and scholarship are "luxury goods," then these economic developments were key to supplying the necessary resources to transform American higher education. For colleges, the growth in national wealth and its increasingly unequal distribution had profound effects.

Through the time of the Civil War, Britain was the leading economic power in the world, accounting for more than one-third of the world's manufacturing output and more than 25 percent of world trade. By the 1890s, however, despite the depression of the 1870s, U.S. income per capita exceeded that of the United Kingdom, and by 1913, the United States not only controlled more than 36 percent of world manufacturing, but its per capita income exceeded that of the United Kingdom by 20 percent. Moreover, in the last three decades of the nineteenth century, American industry rose to a position of worldwide *technological* leadership through the distinctive American system of manufactures. It is also vital to note that this virtually unprecedented economic "turnaround" was accompanied by a sharp increase in income inequality, the development of enormous business corporations and trusts, and the increasing social acceptance of the market economy as a self-regulated sphere of activity.

For more than a century, American ingenuity had laid the foundation for these extraordinary economic accomplishments in areas such as steam transport (Robert Fulton) and textiles (Francis Lowell). It was the decades following the Civil War, however, that marked the ascendancy of the United States as the largest and most dynamic economy of the world. The role of higher education in these startling economic developments seems to have been negligible. In the post–Civil War decades, only 1.3 percent of the nation's twenty-four-year-olds were or had been enrolled in higher education. This figure rose to 2.3 percent by the turn of the century.

These latter statistics are a convenient reminder that in this period the American higher education sector was not only very small, but also quite removed from the forces propelling America forward. Indeed, the individual colleges or universities were tiny communities. As late as 1869, for example, the University of Michigan—already more than fifty years old—consisted of eight or nine modest buildings, half of which were individual faculty houses, and a library of less than ten thousand "well-selected" books. At midcentury, the average college faculty numbered about seven! In summary, I am aware of no evidence that would suggest that institutions of higher education played any significant role in the dramatic transformation of the nineteenth-century American economy and American society.

For a long while it was widely believed that some kind of intrinsic American ingenuity was the source of America's comparative advantage. Although so-called American ingenuity undoubtedly played some role, the remarkable economic developments in the nineteenth century were fueled by other more mundane factors, including unusually high domestic investment rates, the spectacular growth in high-productivity manufacturing, a protected home market, investments in transportation and communications infrastructure, cheap energy (by the 1890s the use of energy resources per worker in the United States was twice as high as in Europe), abundant natural resources, high capital-labor ratios, innovative new business organization models, and imported labor. Particularly important was the American development of efficient mass-production industries. This required not only good technology, but also effective and efficient business organizations, good distribution networks, and a capacity to mobilize capital through efficient capital markets. Once again, few of these factors can be attributed to technology, organizational models, or public policies developed within higher education.[3] A century earlier, this had been the situation in Europe, where new discoveries were the result of the interaction of practical commercial challenges with ingenious entrepreneurs and, to some extent, scattered intellectuals often outside higher education.

In America on the eve of the Civil War, the curriculum and role of the antebellum college were, at best, sufficient to help preserve the older traditions and accumulated learning of Western civilization among a very small group of citizens. Many,

---

[3] The decades following the Civil War also witnessed what many economists call "the second industrial revolution" (1860–1900) initiated by a number of seminal discoveries in science and technology, but most particularly the discovery of electricity. While these discoveries were to transform almost all industrial processes in the twentieth century, their actual impact on nineteenth century economic activities was slight. In the nineteenth century there was little that one could call a U.S. Science Policy. Although the U.S. economy was growing and industrializing rapidly, there was little direct federal government investment in science and technology. Indirectly, however, national policies in such areas as patent policy, immigration policy, tariff policy, and infrastructure investment certainly generated economic dividends and encouraged the deployment of new industrial and agricultural technologies.

however, thought of these institutions as largely irrelevant to the aspirations and exciting prospects of the rapidly evolving society. The antebellum colleges would either have to transform themselves or risk remaining on the sidelines of American life.

On the other hand, it is important to note an embryonic development in American higher education that began late in the nineteenth century and centered on the emergence of the engineering disciplines in American colleges and universities. Earlier in the nineteenth century, important engineering tasks in structures (e.g., bridges), machinery (e.g., the steamboat), networks (e.g., the railroad and canals), and processes (e.g., iron works) were undertaken to put in place the infrastructure to support an industrializing economy that spread over a very wide territory. Most of the skills for this task, however, either had been developed abroad or were the result of energetic American craftsmen and entrepreneurs. At the end of the century, however, the American economy faced the enormously challenging task of translating very rapid advances in scientific understanding in areas such as organic chemistry and electromagnetism into economically effective technologies. Beginning in the early years of the twentieth century, the United States' new engineering schools played a very significant role in this respect. Thus, initiatives in establishing departments of chemical and electrical engineering were critical in achieving the practical large-scale industrial implementation of the world's growing knowledge base in physics and chemistry. These new academic enterprises were to play a major economic role in the first half of the twentieth century.

The Federal Government and Science and Technology

The notion that the national interest required the federal government to become a patron of science and education was very much "in the air" even as the U.S. Constitution was being debated. For their time, many of the founders were people of broad learning who took an active interest in the science of the day.

Discussions at the Constitutional Convention included ideas to establish seminaries for the promotion of literature and the arts and sciences, to establish institutions to promote agriculture, commerce, trades, and manufactures, and to grant patents for useful inventions. As we know, only the issue of patents survived the debate. Thus, even amid the birth pangs of the American nation, there was talk of establishing a national university. However, in those initial decades of the young republic, mastering the art of governing and sustaining the nation took precedence over mastering the art of educating the next generation.

As in seventeenth-century Europe, however, American interest in science and scientific activities during the first half of the nineteenth century thrived almost exclusively in the upper classes or under the auspices of specific elite institutions (such as the Royal Society in England, the Prussian Academy of Arts and Sciences in Germany, the American Philosophical Society in Philadelphia, and the American Academy of Arts and Sciences in Boston), and it was within these precincts where the ideas of the Enlightenment and the enthusiasm for new discoveries initially lay. Such interests and concerns were not, however, part of American college life. In the early years of the American republic, science was for the most part a part-time activity and thought of as an amateur occupation. At the beginning of the nineteenth century, it has been estimated, there were only twenty-two full-time scientific positions in the entire country. In addition, the few professorships of chemistry that were available often went to students of law and theology. It seems as if sectarian orthodoxy was the key criterion for a college appointment in science. Interestingly, although the utilitarian aspect of science enjoyed high repute from the beginning, the mechanism for the development and deployment of new ideas had to be imported from abroad or take place in the farmer's field or the shop floor, not in the college or industrial laboratory.

In the first decades of the nineteenth century, ideas again circulated in Washington about the establishment of a national university. Indeed, some of the schemes included a university for both research and instruction. Alas, such ideas never competed successfully for Congress's attention or resources against infrastructure needs such as roads and canals. Moreover, such "national" projects were thought by many to infringe on state's rights.

When John Quincy Adams became president in 1825, for example, he called for the establishment of a national university and the federal patronage of science. Indeed, Adams thought that patronage of science was like building roads and canals: an obligatory responsibility of the federal government. He saw clearly that Europe was making much more scientific progress than America. Yet his ideas went nowhere. During the first thirty years of the nineteenth century, the only significant federally sponsored scientific activity was the very successful Lewis and Clark expedition during Jefferson's administration. Jefferson had been president of the American Philosophical Society, the leading American scholarly society of that time. Nevertheless, the federal government of the time was both unwilling and unprepared to respond to the practical problems of the day with either a basic science policy or with the machinery to address new problems and challenges as they arose. Even geographic surveys had to be organized and implemented in a relatively ad hoc manner.

The many technological innovations of the period remained rooted in the artisan tradition in America. That great early American innovation, the steamboat, for instance, was a product of this tradition. It seems that only pressing practical needs—such as ways to prevent boiler explosions or to locate practical geological or geographic information—piqued the American public's rather sporadic interest in science and technology. The one major exception to this tradition was the practical implementation of the electrical telegraph, which relied on the basic research of Joseph Henry and other physicists. The telegraph was to become critical to the effective operation of the nation's developing rail systems.

The controversy around the establishment of the Smithsonian Institution is very revealing both of attitudes at the time and of subsequent developments. In 1829, James Smithson bequeathed his estate of $500,000 to set up an institution in Washington to provide for the increase and diffusion of knowledge. Years of Congressional wrangling followed this bequest—not only over the question of what to do with the money, but also whether it was appropriate to accept it. Eventually, the Smithsonian Institution was established with the physicist Joseph Henry as its first secretary. Henry's operating principles were, first, that the institution was to benefit the understanding of all mankind, not merely local interests. Second, he wished to emphasize the creation as opposed to the diffusion of knowledge, and, third, the institution would focus on areas not covered by other American institutions. He was decidedly less interested in the acquisition of books or the creation of a museum. The Smithsonian, therefore, was the first public institution in the United States focused on the creation and diffusion of knowledge, both basic and applied. Its future evolution, of course, followed a broader vision.

Although the federal government became ever more involved in scientific and technical issues during the 1840s and 1850s in order to solve practical problems in areas such as navigation and agriculture, no robust institutional framework was developed to sustain such activities on a permanent basis. Although many scientists of the time saw the need to do something to better mobilize the nation's scientific manpower, few public or private patrons emerged during the first half of the nineteenth century. At the same time, one must acknowledge that federal policies in areas such as patents, immigration, trade, and the regulation of business mergers, banks, transportation, and communications did affect positively the rate of innovation and technological progress. On the whole, however, the American republic was making better progress on other fronts.

THE EMERGENCE OF THE "NEW" AMERICAN UNIVERSITY

Given the self-image of the Colonial and early post-Colonial American college, it should not be surprising how marginal an institution it became in the context of nineteenth-century economic, political, and social developments. The Colonial colleges themselves had been established in an effort to preserve a certain vision of higher learning on the "frontier" of Western civilization and to provide the attitudes and skills deemed necessary for the civil service and the clergy. To the founders of these institutions, such objectives dictated a particular adaptation of the humanistic curriculum of the English Renaissance, one focused on the Bible and classical literature that would, it was thought, develop one's mental discipline, provide a passing acquaintance with Western culture, and produce an appropriate character type (one that resisted the base passions and reflected a certain godliness) to staff local governments and churches. The apparent educational theory behind this curriculum assumed that a special moral character and mental discipline was implied by the study and recitation of the linguistic and cultural content of the Bible and classical languages and literature. Perhaps this focus on the classics reflected the idea that civilization's golden era had come in those ancient times, whose virtues we would do well to recall.

From my perspective, the most important element of the Colonial educators' approach is that it placed little emphasis on speculative and critical philosophy. Instead, it preferred rhetoric to logic and focused on the aesthetic qualities of certain carefully selected texts, a particular sense of virtue, moral control, obedience, and deference to authority. In many ways it is astonishing that such an approach managed to sustain itself after the revolutionary period, when the national discourse reflected a general hostility to "received" traditions and authority. Perhaps this is just further testimony to the peripheral nature of higher education at that time. A new kind of republic was being established, but for the leadership of the nation's Colonial colleges, innovation and change were the last things on their minds. Recall that in the seventeenth and eighteenth centuries European universities (to which the colonists looked as models) were also largely irrelevant to the creation and diffusion of knowledge.

The College Library

Symbolic of the transformation of the antebellum college is the extraordinary transformation of the college library in its scope, its role, and its organization. These changes had their roots in events and ideas that can be traced back a good way, but the transformation began gathering force in the last quarter of the nineteenth century and took flight only after World War I.

In many ways the library symbolizes the most important aspirations of the college or university. Moreover, in the United States the university library now has become the most important repository of that part of our cultural patrimony represented by rare books and special collections. Outside the United States, national, regional, and local institutions, academies, and institutes of various kinds play a much more important role in this respect. The antebellum college, however, had little use for a college library that was anything remotely like our current concept of such an institution. To begin with, the collections were very small and access to these collections by students or faculty was very restricted. It has been estimated that by the late 1830s, the libraries of Harvard, Yale, and Princeton together held more than 10 percent of all the volumes in the libraries of American colleges and seminaries, and that they held about 70,000 books, compared to the more than 300,000 held by the Bodleian Library at Oxford, and the 400,000 volumes held in each of the Paris, Munich, and Vatican libraries (Patton 1838). Moreover, the collections were not systematically organized or developed.

Most college collections of this earlier era were shaped by the periodic personal interests of widely scattered donors. Despite this haphazard pattern of collecting, many valuable books became part of university collections during this period. To some extent particular librarians or faculty members took the initiative to acquire books on mathematics and science, usually from the European continent, and books on literature, history, and religion, usually from the United Kingdom. However, these were sporadic initiatives that were not systematically planned or organized in a manner that sustained the activity over a long period of time. As a result, the college library was certainly not a "research" or "scholarly library." Nor was it an "academic library" focused on supporting the various teaching functions. And it certainly was not fully a "connoisseur's library" reflecting the personal obsessions that motivate such accumulations. My own view is that in the "mainstream" academic imagination of the time, the American college library remained a place reserved for books representing the ultimate authority on a rather narrow domain of issues similar to the colleges' equally narrow curriculum. Few saw the library as a living resource for a world of scholarship characterized by a dynamic, ever-changing frontier.

The reason is simple enough: The antebellum college had a totally different view of its role and its objectives than is now the case. First, the curriculum was narrow and not very demanding and the faculty knew what and how they wanted to teach. Moreover, that curriculum did not require students or faculty to consult a wide variety of sources. Recall that in the nineteenth century, American college books were thought useful primarily for their power to reinforce a certain set of values and to strengthen the mind. Neither students nor faculty felt the need to consult alternative authorities on any matter because issues of innovation, self-realization, new discoveries related to the natural world, or alternative views on society's myriad arrangements were not on their minds. When such study—however rare—was conducted, it took place "in the halls," where there were some, but very few, library resources.[4] The notion that university-based scholarship had a responsibility to help move the scholarly frontier forward had not yet taken hold.

There were scattered efforts in some American colleges to create something like a research or scholarly library even in the first half of the nineteenth century. For example, J. T. Kirkland

---

[4] By "the halls," I mean to a wide variety of ad hoc and informal arrangements, from the offices of individual faculty to student political and literary organizations.

(1818), the president of Harvard from 1810 to 1828, had a vision of a college library as a depository of the world's knowledge. So did George Ticknor, a Harvard professor and a key figure in the founding and governance of the Boston Public Library. Other academic leaders and scholars such as Presidents Tappan at Michigan and Wayland at Brown had similar visions. Many of these early initiatives came from those who had firsthand knowledge of the great European libraries, but these progressive efforts, like analogous efforts on the scholarly frontier, did not take hold inside the antebellum college and were often opposed by most faculty.

A few general additional empirical measures may help clarify the situation faced by college libraries in the nineteenth century. In the 1850s, the Harvard library had just five hundred dollars to spend on new materials. Even in 1870, fewer than 200 volumes were purchased, although additional acquisitions came by gift. In 1884, however, Harvard purchased more than 5,500 volumes, almost all from abroad, and gifts of individual collections began to be an even greater source of library growth. Even by the 1890s, however, President Charles Eliot, who at least a decade earlier had described the library as the heart of the university, was advising Harvard's librarian to rely on the Boston Public Library to provide Harvard faculty with research materials! Although it is difficult to assemble accurate data, I estimate that even by 1880, Harvard, Yale, and Princeton each spent an average of only $10,000 a year on book purchases. The estimated budgets were similar at Berkeley and Michigan. By 1900, the acquisitions budget for the Harvard, Yale, and Princeton libraries seems to have grown to about $30,000 for each institution, and by 1920 to about $50,000. The 1920s, of course, witnessed almost exponential growth in the collections of these institutions as the modern research university emerged. The gradual beginning of serious library collections within U.S. colleges and universities resulted not only from the new role they were slowly assuming, but also from a series of events that permitted the establishment of an international book trade, including the desire of aristocratic families to raise cash either because of the loss of privileges or because of the decline in the economic value of their estates.

Even if the antebellum college library contained a very restricted range of material, interests in new ideas did flourish elsewhere in America. We know, for example, that aboard the "tea ships" in Boston harbor in 1773 were London magazines as well as books by Voltaire, Smith, Jean-Jacques Rousseau, Hume, and other contemporary writers destined for the American market. Groups of individuals in antebellum America were concerned with intellectual and scholarly matters, but the antebellum college was not their home nor was it the home for other serious scholars and inventors. Moreover, the antebellum colleges did not anticipate taking on such a role, expecting instead that the learned societies and certain noncollegiate libraries would provide the supportive environment and associated library resources necessary for scholarship.

Thus, although libraries to support scholarship were rare in nineteenth-century America, institutions such as the Astor library, the Boston Public Library, the Peabody Institute, the Newberry Library, the John Carter Brown Library, and later the Morgan, Huntington, and Folger libraries played a very significant role in bringing key cultural resources to America. Moreover, key faculty and university presidents were often very active in the support of these institutions. Hayes McMullen (2000) has collected data on about ten thousand mostly small libraries that had been established in the United States before 1876. In all probability there were many other small community-based libraries that fell below his radar screen. Here, however, the aim of citizen improvement generally overrode the needs of scholarship. Even private philanthropic foundations were often more focused on ensuring that libraries abroad had enough information about America than on raising the scholarly usefulness of American libraries. Americans, it was widely believed, could rely on their special American ingenuity! Nevertheless, with the help of an increasingly well organized web of book dealers, individual collectors, faculty, and scholars were assembling significant collections throughout the nineteenth century. These collections now form a very important cultural patrimony.

Thus, even as a new intellectual life was emerging in the United States and even as faculty members, here and there, began to take modern scholarship seriously, the college libraries, by and large, did not seem to believe it their responsibility to provide the resources to support or encourage this development. On reflection it seems that the college and the college library were, in the view of those who ran them, "sacred" spaces. Their quasi-sacred role, was to graduate students with the "right" values and "right thinking." In this context, the college library contained a small variety of books on selected subjects directly related to the college's rather circumspect role, and, as a result, the books were available only sporadically. The college library collected no newspapers, or indeed any current material. It was loath to collect literature of any era beyond the classical texts of Greece and Rome and texts relating to the Bible and related theological matters. As the nineteenth century wore on, and even as the colleges slowly began to change, the concept of the college library remained relatively static. As a result, students took matters into their own hands by frequenting off-campus reading rooms for access to current issues, and building their own libraries, both privately and collectively, in student-run organizations. Indeed, the faculty who slowly began to assume the role of the scholars/teachers did likewise. Over time the many individual collectors began to assemble the important book collections that would eventually form part of the foundation of the great university libraries now scattered across the country.

The University Transformed

Thus, the antebellum college and its library are best viewed as rather insignificant components of a set of institutional arrangements that were slowly evolving to support an emerging highly industrialized liberal society. The challenge for the Colonial college and its library was to find a way to be a significant part of a radically new set of arrangements in American life. Other American institutions that were more prepared to support the emerging scholarly community's needs for new intellectual resources included the scholarly or learned societies; individual private libraries of students, faculty, and others (including groups of intellectuals and scholars); libraries abroad; and the special libraries supported by other organizations and various branches of the state, local, and federal government. To these, of course, would soon be added the land-grant colleges.

During the last decades of the nineteenth century the antebellum emphasis on order, restraint, and duty was replaced by a more expansive outlook. American society was nurturing a larger vision of itself and its potential. Americans slowly began to think of themselves no longer as a remote outpost of Western civilization, but rather as being partly responsible for its preservation and transformation. New scientific, economic, and intellectual developments and the rapid expansion of publishing across a wide variety of fields required a secularized and expanded curriculum, increased student access, and the addition to the curriculum of science, the agricultural and mechanical arts, a whole body of emerging social sciences, the reconstituted humanities, and a range of professional programs. Access to the contemporary world of scholarship became essential. This, in turn, required a transformation of both the American college and the college library. Key to all these developments was a new faith that tied scientific progress and scholarly developments of all kinds to human progress.

Moreover, the public increasingly saw the government as an instrument of the national will rather than an enemy of freedom. This allowed passage of new governmental acts that radically expanded secondary education and established the land grant colleges. The Hatch Act of 1887 supported a dramatic expansion and secularization of the university and its curriculum. Federal support for higher education skirted constitutional and political barriers by merging federal and state interests through the device of federal grants to states in either land or money. This influential pattern, established earlier in agriculture, came to be known as the new federalism.

In the post–Civil War era, therefore, the role of the American college in society underwent a revolutionary transformation. The college shed its rather medieval outlook and took on, so to speak, the objectives of the Enlightenment, supplemented by a new belief in the source of human progress. At first it was not at all clear which of the nation's institutions would be key to serving the emerging scholarly communities, whose scholarly activity was no longer solely the avocation of the social elite, but a profession open to all. Just what transformation or reconfiguration of the learned societies, the free-standing professional schools, the new national institutions, the Colonial college, or new local institutions would arise to serve this emerging world of scholarship?

As it turned out, the emerging American research universities managed to usurp all of these functions! In this respect, the American research university went much further than its European counterparts. (In England, for example, the professional schools went their own way.) To fulfill all the responsibilities associated with this vastly expanded role required a revolutionary transformation of the university's outlook from curriculum through facilities to the role and responsibilities of the faculty.

To summarize: By the end of the nineteenth century it had become apparent to most observers that if the United States was to sustain its economic leadership, to more fully realize the aspirations of a liberal democracy, and to generate its own cultural patrimony, it would have to transform and expand its educational system. At the primary and secondary school levels this meant the design and implementation of a system of compulsory education. For colleges and universities, this meant the need to embrace the evolving academic disciplines, to shift the focus of their education programs, and to begin to develop more serious and sustained commitments to scholarship. The nation needed more people with advanced training in both the professions and the academic disciplines.

In response to such needs, the American university curriculum moved from its traditional focus on biblical and classical studies—organized around classical languages and literature, philosophy, grammar, rhetoric, recitation, and logic—to a new emphasis on more contemporary languages and literatures (including Shakespeare), science, and a transformed view of natural philosophy, which spawned a whole series of human sciences in addition to the discipline of philosophy itself. Rather quickly, a pedagogical evolution took place. The recitation was replaced by the lecture and the seminar and the curriculum was reorganized around specialized disciplines within the natural sciences, the evolving social sciences, and the reconstituted, reconceptualized, and expanded humanities.

Analogous transformations had to take place in virtually all scholarly and research venues within the university. With respect to libraries, for example, not only would the collections have to be dramatically enlarged, cared for, and reorganized, but new services would have to be provided and new facilities put in place.

I want to focus now on one of the central liberal ideas of the Enlightenment and what it has meant for America's colleges and universities, because a commitment to it has created tensions between society and the transformed university, which, to this day, are not always appreciated. The political and social attitude that necessarily underlies a liberal society supports free thinking and open futures and is always looking for a better configuration of societal arrangements. In short, this attitude is hostile to comfort with the status quo. This hostility has a number of dramatic but straightforward implications for scholarship and higher education. First, the attitude of a liberal society is, in some way, a call to arms for scholarship and discovery of all kinds. It requires a whole new portfolio of resources and incentives—both economic and social—including, for example, new types of laboratories and libraries for the colleges and emerging universities.

The truly startling development in the last decade of the nineteenth century was that American society decided to supply such resources to higher education even in the face of the university's new role as critic of the existing arrangements in science and society. A public financing its own critics certainly is unusual and reflects a rather deep commitment to the liberal idea that all current understandings and arrangements need to be replaced as we create a better world. Despite this dedication to the liberal ideal of maintaining a certain uneasiness about the status quo, many citizens, even today, continue to look to authority and tradition as a source of both freedom and comfort, and to view change as the omen of loss and estrangement.

Historically speaking, public support of institutions of higher education that serve both as society's servant and as its critic represents one of the latest of the social and political revolutions of the liberal enlightenment. It is no foregone conclusion that the public will continue to believe that the education and research programs of the contemporary university provide a valuable social product worth the financial investments and risks involved. I myself find it quite astonishing that our society has remained committed to generously support, honor, and respect a set of institutions designed, in part, to be critical of the very arrangements within which most key decision makers have prospered.

The American Model

As I mentioned previously, one of the common misunderstandings regarding the transformation of American higher education concerns the influence of the new German university. Although the German model did have a very significant influence—especially on the nature of the university's commitment to scholarship in both the sciences and the humanities—its influence is often exaggerated.[5] What developed in America had not only strong affinities to a number of different educational traditions, but also a strong utilitarian perspective. The resulting set of institutions has a very distinctively American flavor. For example, the sharp separation within a single institution of graduate education, undergraduate education, and professional education is a distinctively American innovation, as is the sustained focus on the benefits of a liberal education; the identification of the Ph.D. degree as a research degree; the more or less peaceful coexistence of public and private liberal arts colleges, research universities, and state and community colleges; and the incorporation of professional schools into the university. Likewise, the role of university faculty within the American research university is a special combination of the German and British models, each distinctively adapted to the American context. In the area of governance, as I have already noted, the American model, with its community-based boards and with a great deal of decision-making power delegated to the faculty through the president, is quite distinctive.

In summary, the particular institutional structure of the modern American university emerged from the Colonial colleges, from land-grant colleges, and from a set of new private universities, as well as from a complex set of influences. These influences included not only different European models (German, French, and British) but also some distinctively American needs and traditions such as the rather universalistic outlook of liberal Protestantism; a cultural preference for meritocracy; a commitment to increasing our material welfare; a certain kind of egalitarianism; immigration; industrialization; and the economic forces emanating from a rapidly industrializing nation whose economy was organized around private markets.

[5] Keen observers such as Daniel Gilman (the "founder" of John Hopkins) and Richard Ely (a distinguished economist and one of the founders of the American Economic Association) were emphatic about the need to construct an American model that would not and could not be a simple copy of the German one.

As for the German model, it is often forgotten that one aspect of German higher education in the nineteenth century emphasized the cultivation of the mind and the spirit and the formation of character in line with certain classical notions of wisdom and virtue. After all, one of the important characteristics of the Enlightenment was a new focus on the importance of the well-ordered inner life and psychological structure of the individual. German educators hoped that higher education would play a key role in helping to develop a certain character type. Autonomy required, among other things, self-control. Such a focus was also very much part of the objective of a liberal education in the English-speaking countries at the time and has remained so in the United States. In Germany, however, the strongest intellectual current was a search for an intellectual ordering of the world and the celebration of the freedom achieved through a focus on reason and the search for truth. Although Alexander Humboldt himself had a more humanistic conception of the modern university, the focus on the search for new knowledge won out as the primary organizing principle supporting the contemporary European university. These same forces played themselves out in America in an analogous, but somewhat different manner.

Thus, although the development of the new German university was an important source of inspiration for American education reformers, a distinctively American model emerged as their plans necessarily responded to American conditions and a wide variety of American cultural attitudes and political realities. The overwhelming motive of those guiding the transformation of American higher education was to improve the existing colleges by reinventing or transforming them—not by simply emulating the German, French, or British universities about which they had rather limited knowledge. The emergence of the twentieth-century American university is best thought of as a century-long struggle, not only to redefine the American college, but also to improve it.

Two principal themes were operating in this overall desire to redefine and improve the American college. One rather utilitarian theme stressed instruction in modern languages, mathematics (especially applied mathematics), and the emerging sciences. The other theme, which grew more directly out of the classical tradition and emphasized history, literature, and the fine arts in addition to the classics, continued to prize the formation of character and intellect rather than direct "usefulness"; it advocated the preservation of some overall unity in the curriculum. This latter theme has formed the backbone of the continued cultural commitment to a liberal arts education in America, though it has played a much smaller role in the development of contemporary European higher education.

In any case, the "utilitarian" ideal moved toward the specialization of knowledge and, along with the increased popularity of electives, was thought to connect the college to the real world. The liberal arts model, on the other hand, resented specialization, insisting that the undergraduate curriculum focus on the integration of knowledge and culture as well as the accumulation of needed expertise. Its aim remained "the ideal citizen" and/or preparation for advanced training in a specialty. In a certain way, the liberal arts tradition in America gained added strength from the Victorian crisis of religious faith, which encouraged the search for new sources of cultural unity and a spiritual vision to replace the loosening glue of the belief in God.[6]

Of course, other tensions in the system overlapped with these two principal themes. The controversy continued between those committed to specialization and those believing that knowledge at the deepest level reflects a unified whole. The sides in this debate had different views on curriculum and the scholarly agenda. The tension between the sacred and the secular continued, as did the associated struggle between those who thought the sacred

[6] As we shall see in the next essay, central to Cardinal Newman's midcentury defense and definition of the university was a separation of the sacred and the secular into two different intellectual spheres.

and the secular formed two independent spheres and those who thought that the sacred and the secular would eventually be shown to derive from a single intellectual framework. There was the tension between those who thought the aim of the curriculum was to develop the knowledge base and cognitive abilities of the student, and those who thought that higher education should also produce the kind of citizen who shared a certain habit of mind and outlook with other educated people and leaders.

More specifically, however, there was about to be an abrupt shift in federal policy toward higher education. It was slowly becoming apparent to policy makers that if the growth of American industrial strength was to be sustained, the educational system would need substantial reform and public investment. Although the first Morrill Land Grant College Act was passed in 1862 (thanks largely to the fact that Southern representatives had stopped attending sessions of Congress), little research activity developed until the Hatch Act of 1887, which provided each state with funding for agricultural experiment stations. Despite these important initial efforts, science in America at the beginning of the twentieth century remained behind that of Europe even after the American economy had surpassed all those in Europe.

On the other hand, by the turn of the century, government at all levels was increasing its investments in "new" colleges and universities, American industry was building its own technological infrastructure, and the formation of private trusts was beginning to have an effect on colleges and universities. For example, in the wake of the great merger wave (1897–1902) came the establishment of the great corporate research centers by industrial giants such as Kodak, Du Pont, AT&T, and General Electric. Edison's Menlo Park, New Jersey, "invention factory" had come somewhat earlier (1878).[7] Only in the chemical industry had

[7] In the 1920s, some of the major "industrial" foundations lost interest in the support of traditional charities and began to look to science to solve society's problems. They began to support basic scientific research, demonstration projects to test various propositions, scientific education, the professional organizations of scientists, and research institutions. This blurred the distinction be-

there been any substantial use of scientifically trained personnel prior to the turn of the century.

Within higher education, the expansion and redefinition of the curriculum that resulted from the need for the development of new skills and new concepts of what it meant to be educated was accompanied by a substantial delegation of power to the faculty; the expansion, reorganization, and reassembly of the academic disciplines; and the slow institutionalization of extramural scholarly programs, especially in science and engineering. The civic function of higher education in America increasingly was seen as requiring: (1) the incorporation of engineering, basic and applied sciences, and other specialized expertise into university faculties and curricula; (2) the professionalization and empowerment of all faculties; (3) the development of a full disciplinary structure for both programs and governance; and (4) the adoption of new organizing principles that focused on the development of new knowledge, graduate as well as undergraduate education, and a more critical and discerning understanding of our society and its beliefs. Finally, educators slowly backed away from the notion that there was no morality without religion and began a search to locate alternative principles that might govern our relations with one another. It was, if you like, an enthusiastic return to the scholastic impulse, within the economic, social, and political context of an emerging liberal democracy.

The small, paternalistic antebellum college, with its limited and circumspect resources, its concerns for the piety and morality of students, and its curriculum centered on classical languages and literature, gave way to the larger and more secular university and it did so in a manner that also transformed the meaning and nature of professional education and its relationship to the university. Most surprising about this development was the relatively novel idea that new scholarship and the capac-

---

tween government and private institutions in a manner that never happened abroad. This diffused power eventually allowed private organizations to play a bigger role in science and science policy.

ity to innovate might be an immensely practical requirement for sustaining economic growth and pursuing other social goals. These notions, together with other American traditions, led to the model of the modern American research university as a highly decentralized system devoted to mass, if not universal, education in the context of a constantly renewed search for new ideas and understandings.

As I have already noted, the notion that the state and other establishment interests could benefit from a set of independent higher educational institutions characterized by free and open debate about science and society is rather astonishing. This role of the university as society's critic has often created tensions between the university and its sponsors, as Clark Kerr certainly experienced at the University of California in the 1950s and 1960s. At times over the last decades the political mobilization of students and faculty seems to have upset the equipoise between the research university and its sponsors and has threatened to undermine support for the enterprise. Many claim this to have been the case in the late 1960s and early 1970s. During the "McCarthy era" in the early 1950s, it seemed to many in the academic community that independent political ideas were no longer going to be tolerated on the nation's campuses. Nevertheless, over time the American research university has been one of the principal producers of new ideas regarding how the status quo might be altered, whether in science, culture, or politics. Most telling of all, over long periods of time and for a wide variety of reasons, public and private support for the research university has continued to grow.

Science, Religion, and Higher Education

Despite the important changes that characterized American higher education in the late nineteenth century, especially its increasingly secular outlook, most educational leaders in America continued to believe in the close connection between religion and truth. Although some college presidents, such as Cornell's

Andrew Dickson White, were outspoken in their belief that science and religion were at odds with each other, the more common view among university and community leaders was the traditional theme of natural theology: that one could come to know God through nature. Most educational leaders believed (or hoped) that a deeper commitment to scholarship might uncover a single truth that would have mutually supporting spiritual, moral, and cognitive dimensions. In this respect they echoed sentiments expressed at the dawn of modern science in the seventeenth century by figures such as Bacon and Boyle. Robert Boyle (1670), for example, believed that the study of nature would lead to a greater understanding of God's creation and a greater appreciation of humankind's responsibility to care for God's great work. In such a context, scientific investigations could be considered acts of religious devotion because they provided new evidence of the divine order, revealing that nature and scripture were part of the same truth. Francis Bacon had the idea of locating the basis of science in God's laws, as embodied in nature. Therefore, from a Christian perspective science was an ethically respectable activity. This religious tradition encouraged individuals to overcome deficiencies, to be a force for social change, or to enhance one's moral sensibilities—all callings that are remarkably similar to aspects of the so-called liberal-secular outlook. At the very least, many hoped that some grand intellectual structure would emerge that provided a place for both science and religion. Some continued to hold on to the notion that God would not allow any contradiction between His words (scripture) and His deeds (nature).

Francis Bacon had the notion that the personal characteristics necessary for success were the same virtues extolled by the Church. This general notion continues to occupy an important place in the minds of some contemporary scientists. For example, the distinguished scientist Francis Collins (1995), the director of the Human Genome Project, has written: "For the scientist who is also Christian science is a form of worship. It is the uncovering of the incredible, awesome beauty of God's creation." In any case, it is clear from public records that university leaders of the late nineteenth and early twentieth centuries such as Woodrow Wilson of Princeton and James Burril Angell of Michigan did not intend, as is often claimed, that their reforms should banish morality or religion from higher education. Rather, they continued to believe, or hope, that the new scholarly approaches would improve our understanding of all knowledge, scientific and religious. Better knowledge, they hoped, would produce better (i.e., more religious) people. They believed that the development of reason was a special ally in this project because reason was the wellspring of thrift, education, hard work, and devotion to religious duties. Therefore, religion could be considered part of a liberal education. Moreover, the loss of theistic beliefs seemed to them to leave no basis for the establishment of an alternative morality. These university presidents seem to have had little awareness that faith in the divine might be replaced by faith in reason, science and progress.

In Britain during the last half of the nineteenth century, science evoked great controversy, even anguish. Insecurity was fueled by social change, revolutions abroad, and the erosion of elements of religious faith by new discoveries in geology, astronomy, and biology. Most important, these scientific findings seemed to threaten the centrality of the human being and the planet Earth in the divine plan. Moreover, the close association of scientists and philosophers began to break down as natural philosophy gave way under the weight of specialization. Scientists became less concerned with questions of ultimate truth and universal values. Scientific materialism replaced the scientific search for a universal framework. Equally shattering was Darwin's notion of the lack of any purpose in the Darwinian scheme. This swept away the divine plan for some. Others, however, continued to believe that a better knowledge of nature would engender a deeper love of and respect for the creator, despite the need to put aside certain truth claims. As Charles Kingsley, the noted English author and clergyman, is said to have remarked, "I am sure that science and the creeds will shake hands at last . . . and by God's

79

grace I may help them do so." Few believed, however, that ultimate matters of faith could be resolved by science, or that science could ever be the measure of all things or provide full meaning to our lives.

The unity of knowledge approach assumes that ethics and the sacred are forms of knowledge not qualitatively distinguishable from other forms of knowledge such as physics and chemistry. It is sharply different from Cardinal Newman's mid-nineteenth-century approach, which, in defending the role of theological studies in the university, separated the sacred (human purpose, ultimate meaning, and moral values) from the secular (facts about the natural world) and thus detached secular knowledge from the values of the sacred sphere and may have led to the banishment of the sacred from the increasingly secular university.

In the late nineteenth and early twentieth centuries, however, skepticism became the operative scholarly principle, and this limited the possibility for religious truths to be grounded in scientific claims. Nevertheless, many scientists of the day continued to think that their work would help establish certain divine principles. Moreover, the new humanities (concerned with the inner life of human consciousness and sensibility) did not easily accept the notion that knowledge could no longer be based on religious claims to universal truths. Few anticipated Walter Lippmann's remarkable suggestion in the *New Republic* in 1966 that society had finally become "emancipated and thus deprived of the guidance and support of traditional and customary authority—[and, therefore,] there has fallen to the universities a unique, indispensable and capital function in the intellectual and spiritual life of modern society." The pioneering reformers of American higher education did not intend or believe that faith in the process of secular inquiry would ever rise above "mere" religious and ethnic sectarianism and end up setting beliefs that defined the nature of the good life or the good society. Indeed, at the dawn of the twentieth century it continued to be assumed that America was a Christian nation, indeed a Protestant nation, and that its public policies ought to reflect this fact. Moreover, theologians continued to play a role, as they had for centuries, in the American world of ideas.

As the claims of scripture ran up against new evidence regarding, for example, the age of the universe, scientists began restricting their investigations to natural phenomena and ignoring the formulation of events as described in the Bible. More important, scientific work became theologically neutral in the sense of being compatible with both theism and atheism alike and, therefore, separated from theology. Before long it seemed to many that scientific knowledge was more useful than speculation, faith tradition, and authority. Even the so-called human sciences were affected as observers began to treat human affairs as objects of scientific analysis rather than of philosophical speculation. In this context, many social reformers began to believe that the new social sciences would help solve real social problems and were, therefore, an authentic and preferred religious vocation. The accumulation of empirical knowledge, they began to think, would be a faster route to social reform than religious devotion. In the end, specialization and the emphasis on ongoing inquiry replaced the religious and theoretical presuppositions that had given coherence to the antebellum collegiate curriculum.

As the Christian faith and worldview began to lose its place as the foundation for the intellectual life of the American college, some unifying concept was required to take its place. How could one ensure a body of coherent knowledge if the curriculum was severed from religious belief? What would substitute for the old unifying concept of moral philosophy? In America, the emerging social sciences and the newly reconstituted humanities (focusing on the interplay between text and historical context) took up this responsibility. Together they began to provide a framework that gave some coherence to a liberal arts curriculum in which the dictates of Christian theology and the imperatives of religious faith no longer seemed quite so compelling. Meanwhile, the sciences and the scientific approach provided this increasingly secular environment with some substitute for the claims of faith because, as I have already noted, they seemed to encourage the same personal characteristics—truth telling, patience, hard work, open-mindedness, perseverance, and independent thinking—as the object of a new and expanded notion of a liberal education. Indeed, just such claims, together with the earlier suggestion that science would help reveal God's plan, enabled scientists to gain a rather early influence on colleges and universities that were being quickly reconstituted. In time, the deepening of liberal democratic values that emphasized both the autonomy and the worth of each individual and the future as the bearer of greater possibilities transformed the basis of university life. The university was no longer the intellectual and moral arm of a quasi-established church. Now neither the church nor the college president could claim to represent the life of the mind in the new American university.

Perhaps this transition was also helped by a new national rhetoric that took the language of religious faith and transferred it to the defense of a new faith in liberal democracy. Indeed, leaders began to speak of democracy as the very expression of our humanity, as a sacred trust we must pass on to others as well as to future generations. Our devotion to this new faith may have helped many in a time of transition to a more secular society, but it carried the risk of all faiths: the absence of doubt. Indeed, it seemed to become almost sinful to question the assumptions of liberal democracies—for example, that all citizens are capable of governing themselves, are self-reliant, and are patriotic.

Despite the widespread notion that science and religion are always in conflict, history reveals a much more varied and complex relationship. In fact, there have been many eras when science and religion worked in close alliance with one another in order to deepen our understanding of scripture or to help establish the existence of God. At other times, science and religion demonstrated a simple indifference to each other. In the contemporary public imagination, however, it is the conflicts between science and religion such as those that surrounded the work of Copernicus, Galileo, and Darwin that provide the normal paradigm for the uneasy or mutually aloof relationship between science and religion. Moreover, as I understand it, the present-day position of the Catholic Church, for example, affirms both the constrained autonomy of science and its separation from theology. In this view, natural or scientific knowledge can never contradict knowledge revealed through God's messengers, but neither can the scriptures be taken as a guide to nature. In addition, many philosophers now hold that it is not possible to infer moral obligations from scientific discoveries. At the current time, therefore, as Cardinal Newman asserted in the mid-nineteenth century, many consider theology and science to be independent of each other. For most American university leaders early in the twentieth century, however, it seemed quite possible that a new era of cooperation between religion and science was ahead of them.

One final irony that characterized the emergence of the twentieth-century American university was the divorce from a university context of what had once been perhaps a central purpose of the antebellum college: the professional preparation of the clergy. The uneasy status of religion in U.S. public life, and its very pluralism, meant that this training, unlike the professional education of lawyers, doctors, and a myriad of other professions, would for the most part take place outside the university.

CONCLUSION

It is interesting to note that the modern American corporation, the movement to standardize the training of professional workers, and the modern American university all arose simultaneously at a time when society was searching for new or reconstituted social and cultural institutions. At the same time, the American university transformed itself without ever having developed a unifying intellectual language of its own or a well-articulated vision for the structure that developed. American undergraduate, graduate, and professional schools were brought together into a single institution, but without any clear and systematic idea of how they might relate to one another. In place of such a vision, it seems to me, the American university, along with many other cultural organizations, adopted the language and to some extent the structure of America's business organizations. Although this language and structure (e.g., productivity, priorities, hierarchical organization, and departments) served many useful purposes, it tended to obscure the special communal nature of university life and to accentuate the specialization of the disciplines and the separation of the undergraduate, graduate, and professional programs. The American university continues to struggle with this reality as it strives to sustain conversations among cultures and across generations. Only through such conversations will we be better able to understand each other and ourselves.

In this respect, it is interesting to recall that the eighteenth-century language of globalization was often the language of faith and the devotional sermon. The newly interconnected world was often the subject of sermons of that day, which ranged from Jeremiad-like critiques of luxury occasioned by the importation of exotic goods from Bengal to comparisons of the Popish French to the "innocent" Protestant imperialists.

The underlying problem today is that the language of private markets and business corporations does not provide a compelling alternative framework to the hierarchy of accepted virtues of an earlier period, to subsequent notions regarding the primacy of Western culture, or to the bonds of common religious commitments that tied together the higher education community for so long. Moreover, the challenge of sustaining the communal character of the world of scholarship and education is aggravated by the continued separation and growth of the new disciplines, along with the increased technicality and special language of each. In an environment where it is more and more difficult to sustain the communal character of our lives, we must ask ourselves: Who will concern themselves with the larger shape of things? What is the meaning of disciplines operating in an intellectually and educationally decontextualized environment? These prospects were already considered troublesome during the

birth of the modern American university, and the problem remains. Perhaps they are what concerned John Dewey, who
wanted to ground the entire educational effort in the language
of "actual" people.

As we look back from the perspective of the first years of the
twenty-first century, we can see that the American high school
never became a sufficient preparation for students wanting to
begin specialized work immediately on entering the university.
Some believe this turned out to be less of a problem than one
might have feared because it prevented the contemporary American university from becoming what they believe are the overspe-
cialized and Balkanized structures of our European counterparts.

All revolutions or significant transformations are best thought
of as the hybrid results of competing visions, rather than the
complete realization of any single idea or approach. As American higher education moved toward the twentieth century, a
number of views regarding its evolution operated simultaneously, often in combination or in conflict with one another.
Moreover, a number of different practical approaches can be
derived from any single grand vision. To begin implementing
the grand vision requires negotiations among those who hold
competing views. What actually gets done depends not only on
the overall appeal of the various visions being proposed, but also
the structure of the various decision-making bodies and the
"larger" alignment of political, social, and economic forces. One
of the reasons why new or previously "marginal" institutions
often take the lead in times of significant change is that during
such times many of the barriers to implementing a new vision
are lower.

In the broader U.S. context, public policies, for example, are
usually a patchwork of ideas, and not the realization of a single
vision. Indeed, this type of outcome is virtually assured, given
the distinct influences, practices, schedules, and traditions of
Congress, the executive branch, and the courts in matters of public policy. In higher education, it is no accident that the U.S.
system is composed not only of separate though interacting pub-

lic and private sectors, but also a public sector that allows for the possibility of a number of distinct approaches. In my view, this type of patchwork outcome results from a typically American attitude that distrusts authority—especially authority with a potentially wide span of control and influence. Although this outcome is often described as the result of an overall consensus, in fact the process of transformation of the American university was hardly uniform and has generated a patchwork quilt of different types of institutions that became the American "system" of higher education.

On an even broader scale, even if one believes that a basic commitment to liberalism (i.e., private property, rationality, progress, individual liberty) is the ultimate constraint within which all American institutions operate, there are many different versions of liberalism. My own view is that in the United States, one of the most basic liberal commitments is to organizing economic activity around private markets. At its best, this is believed to both facilitate individual freedom and growth and expand the wealth of the nation. In turn, private property rights are considered necessary to allow these markets to operate effectively. Controversy continues, however, regarding how to recognize a market failure and what to do about it. Likewise, controversy persists over the perceived shortcomings of institutions of higher education and how to rectify them.

As we struggle to understand the history of the transformation of the antebellum college, we ourselves are in the midst of a revolution in information technology that is certain to transform many aspects of how information is created, filtered, assigned a category, preserved or discarded, and stored. This revolution will undoubtedly affect American higher education in ways we cannot today imagine. Moreover, the set of institutions and institutional arrangements eventually assigned to these tasks may be quite different than those that we now take for granted. During the last century, the university became an ever more dominant institution in preserving aspects of our cultural heritage for future generations while outlining a new future in science and society.

Will this comprehensive role continue in the coming decades, or will this new technological environment generate a different set of institutions?

The late nineteenth century was not the last period to witness a transformation in American higher education. The twentieth century witnessed an almost dizzying metamorphosis in American colleges and universities. It saw the higher education sector grow much faster than anyone expected, the links between higher education and society become more varied and complex, and the influence of the state increase dramatically. Older institutions expanded and changed, and newer institutions not only helped meet the increasing demand for access to higher education, but often provided the intellectual leadership necessary to meet a whole new set of aspirations. In some sense, the century witnessed a transformation from an "elite" system to a "mass" system of higher education. However, the century of Lenin, Winston Churchill, Joseph Stalin, Franklin Roosevelt, Adolf Hitler, the Cold War, Sigmund Freud, Albert Einstein, Francis Crick, and James Watson has drawn to a close. New challenges to the human condition are arising: the challenges of demography, the national and international distribution of income, new infectious diseases, new forms of communications, the environment, new technologies, political and cultural fragmentation amid forces pressing for globalization, and even challenges to the role of rationality in helping us achieve a better understanding of the human experience. Indeed, it is hard to avoid the feeling that we are on the brink of another transformation.

Liberal Education, Liberal Democracy, and the Soul of the University

That man, I think, has had a liberal education, who has
been trained in youth that his body is the ready servant of
his will, and does with ease and pleasure all the work
that, as a mechanism, it is capable of; whose intellect is a
clear, cold logic engine, to be turned to any kind of work,
and spin the gossamers as well as forge the anchors of the
mind; whose mind is stored with knowledge of the great
and fundamental truths of Nature and of the laws of her
operations; one who, no stunted ascetic, is full of life and
fire, but whose passions are trained to come to heel by a
vigorous will, the servant of a tender conscience; who has
learned to love all beauty, whether of Nature or of art, to
hate all vileness, and to respect others as himself.
T. Huxley (1934, p. 141)

I HOPE in this essay to remove some of the accumulated debris that has distorted our common memory and thus has hampered our clear perception of the evolving nature and role of a liberal education and its relationship to professional education, moral education, and liberal democracy, and our understanding of who has the ongoing responsibility to protect the soul of the university. Despite the importance of these issues, they take up relatively little space in our national discourse on the current and future state of higher education in America. Currently, they exist as a kind of backdrop to topical controversial issues such as the appropriate form of affirmative action policies and the impact of online learning and perennial issues such as the tension between teaching and research, the fair allocation of research costs, overall costs, tuition levels, and access. These remain critically important matters, but I and others have addressed these concerns many times. On the other hand, we often forget not only that the social functions of the American research university are grounded in the ideals of the Enlightenment, but also that the continuing vitality of the research university is dependant on our society's continuing commitment to the virtues of scientific mindedness, technical and material progress, liberal democratic politics, toleration, and both moral and political pluralism.

My overall perspective can be briefly summarized. First, although the desirability of a liberal education remains an important aspect of our national discourse on higher education, it is not a well-defined concept and, if properly understood, it is only indirectly related to the various curricular debates of the last few decades. Indeed, our discourse in this arena seldom distinguishes between the "liberal arts" as a curriculum, a particular way to organize knowledge, and the "liberal arts" as a vehicle to support our notions of ideal citizenship in a pluralistic liberal democracy. New paradigms and practices are needed for learners at all levels. If we are to articulate a new organizing idea to guide developments in the liberal arts, we must begin by clarifying the meanings and objectives of liberal learning. Second, the current rather rigid separation between undergraduate education and graduate and professional education is ill advised and serves to undermine the appropriate objectives of both a liberal education and a professional education. Indeed, the philosophy of a liberal arts education presumes learning experiences that enable citizens to understand their interrelated social, moral, and professional responsibilities. This view is as central to high-quality professional education as to education in the arts and sciences. Third, all these presumptions regarding liberal education and one of its key products—liberal learning—are intimately tied to the nature of the liberal democracy, which provides the political and social structure for our lives.

Democracy may be one of the most demanding of political arrangements in that it requires political responsibility from all citizens. In an ideal sense, liberal democracy requires all citizens to have an informed cultural awareness and a capacity for critical judgment. Democracy further requires a certain degree of participation, the assumption of responsibilities, respect for different views, moral awareness, respect for others, and commitment to some kind of equality, tolerance, and procedural justice. To me, a liberal education is directly connected to the nature of the society we wish to sustain. When I think about education, I think about the ideal human types for the society we envision. It is not simply what we teach, or even what our students learn, but what kind of persons they become that really matters. We must think, therefore, about what kind of person, what kind of skills, and what goals should characterize that society, and only then inquire just what type of education or scholarly agenda contributes to these goals. Otherwise, education could be considered a private indulgence that, whatever its value to an individual, does not deserve public support.

A particularly important quality of liberal learning is the ability to imagine how we are all to live together in a peaceful, mutually empathetic and supportive manner in the face of a wide variety of different beliefs about substantive moral issues and the empirical state of the world. We face this particular challenge with some widely accepted rules for settling disagreements about the empirical state of the world, but also with the knowledge that our mechanisms for resolving social and moral disagreements are only imperfect and evolving. The fact is that a "best" solution to many of the important challenges we face cannot be identified. Ambiguity, uncertainty, and anxiety are therefore our constant companions as we try to build a better future.

The extraordinary success of the contemporary scientific enterprise has succeeded in both increasing and diminishing our sense of wonder and awe regarding nature. It has encouraged us to believe in our capacity to fashion artifacts both to control almost any aspect of our environment and to provide for our every need. Whether correct or not, this belief has the undesirable side effect of encouraging us to see life's challenges as having well-defined solutions, whether on the personal or the public policy level. The fact is that despite the extraordinary scientific accomplishments of recent decades, we hardly know ourselves or what we are to become. Given this uncertainty regarding the empirical state of the world and our disagreements and moral philosophies, defining our ethical obligations to others will be an ongoing and controversial struggle.

Indeed, both inside and outside higher education, we remain uneasy about our moral and political responsibilities, about who we have to obey, and on what issues such obedience is required. For example, we are uncertain who in higher education has the authority to decide on the nature and curriculum of educational institutions, or what the limits should be on this authority. Not only do we have no morally acceptable way to reach full agreement on the structure and objectives of our various institutions of higher education, but we Americans have no strong desire to search hard for such a consensus. Instead we rely on a set of mixed strategies reflecting different perspectives that serve to limit the outright conflict over educational matters. This typically American strategy is thought to protect our freedom of action, preserve options, and even promote social justice and efficiency. It does not, of course, eliminate all conflict, because educational institutions, like other important social institutions, are not infinitely diffuse or divisible.

LIBERAL EDUCATION: WHAT IS IT AND IS IT AN OLD OR A NEW IDEA?

For almost two thousand years, the idea of a liberal education has attracted the attention and loyalty of thoughtful educators, scholars, and citizens concerned with higher education. Indeed, few educational ideals have attracted more adherents, sustained more controversy, and had more "staying power" than this concept. For centuries, educators, scholars, and citizens across a broad range of the political, social, and cultural spectrum have urged colleges and universities to meet their civic responsibility of providing a curriculum that fulfills the imperatives of a liberal education. This consistent devotion to an educational ideal is all the more remarkable given the enormous and continuing growth in our stock of knowledge and the changing notion of what the word *liberal* implies.

Although the term *liberal education* is an old and even venerable one, most contemporary discourse seems to accept Cardinal Newman's notion that a liberal education is a form of learning that has no sequel or aspiration or objective beyond itself. This seems close in spirit to the idea Plato had for his Academy, namely, that it was a place for matters removed from daily cares and tasks. As I understand Cardinal Newman, such an education would nevertheless provide the student with personal attributes such as self-knowledge, wisdom, and the judgment to be a responsible citizen. This concept has at least the great advantage of defining a liberal education as distinctly different than a professional education.

Equally significant is that Cardinal Newman, like Alexander von Humboldt before him, elevates the prestige and importance of the arts and sciences faculties. For Humboldt, this was primarily the result of the increasing importance of the disciplines, whereas for Cardinal Newman, the liberal arts or their result— liberal learning—were simply a more important aspect of education than the more practical and focused activities of the various professional schools. In this latter respect, however, he treated theology as a special case, clearly separating knowledge from faith. Cardinal Newman's separation was meant to defend the sacred realm from scientists. In Cardinal Newman's time, the more common approach was to treat the sacred as a form of knowledge that, although separate, was not qualitatively distinguishable from other forms of knowledge and was equally available to human conceptualization. However, as I have noted, the acceptance of Cardinal Newman's separation has resulted in the virtual banishment of the sacred from an increasingly secular university. Indeed, over time the moral imperatives of education have been increasingly replaced by the single idea of objectivity, which, whatever else its benefits, has lent great status to the disciplines and given them a great deal more independence from community views.

Although the Greeks are credited with articulating the basic components of the liberal arts, even they had several different educational strategies. One focused on literature, another on the search for truth and new understanding, yet another on the training of effective civic leaders. It was the Romans who coined the phrase *septem artes liberales* (the seven liberal arts: grammar, rhetoric, logic, arithmetic, geometry, music, and astronomy). This did not lead Roman educators, however, to adopt a coherent curriculum based on these subjects. Indeed, Roman society also included a number of approaches to higher education curricula with greatly different emphases. Indeed, Cicero (in *De republica*, IV, 15) wrote that the educational curriculum should not adhere to any strict rules or be applied uniformly to all. For Thomas Aquinas in late medieval Europe, a liberal education included, besides the *septem artes liberales*, natural philosophy, moral philosophy, and metaphysics. As time passed, however, additional objectives for a liberal education were developed, such as the freeing of the individual from the authority of previous ideas, the disinterested search for truth, the pursuit of alternative ideas, and the development and integrity of the individual and of his or her power of reason. This expansion of the liberal education agenda was a natural development as society's educational requirements expanded and evolved over time.

Thus the classical societies of Greece and Rome, European societies of the Renaissance, nineteenth-century Europe and Britain, and Colonial and contemporary America have all had their own quite distinct understandings of the purposes of a liberal education. Not surprisingly, these distinctions usually reflected contending social and cultural commitments (e.g., Hellenism versus Christianity, reason versus revelation) as well as distinct views of both the source of new wisdom and the role of institutions of higher education. Most important, although the concept of a liberal education goes back to classical times, so too does the controversy over its structure and purposes. Indeed, alternative approaches to both the theory and practice of liberal education have been a constant source of tension in educational thinking for two millennia. These tensions appear in ancient Greek sources (e.g., the Sophists vis-à-vis Socrates and Plato) and in the wisdom literature of the Old Testament, as well as in medieval times and down to the present. Fortunately, such continuing tensions are normally a healthy sign that higher education is responding to important social and political change.

Despite this history of controversy, change, and evolution, the pursuit of the amorphous ideal of a "liberal education" remains an article of faith in much of higher education. This continuing "devotion" has been bought at the price of continuously expanding the constellation of ideas accommodated by the term *liberal education*. Thoughtful educators now use the venerable term to include everything from a narrow focus on the "old" or "new" canon of "great" texts to a serious in-depth study of a particular liberal arts subject. The catalogue of liberal arts subjects, now greatly expanded beyond the trivium and quadrivium, includes all of the burgeoning sciences. Within at least some academic circles, however, the incorporation of the theoretical and experimental sciences into the curriculum remains incomplete. For some, the literary and philosophical traditions that replaced the near monopoly of the classical curriculum still retain a special stature. In any event, the label *liberal education* applies both to educational curricula that prescribe students' choices and to those that leave all such choices to students. It incorporates all manner of pedagogies and embraces approaches that emphasize breadth of knowledge and those that emphasize depth within a relatively narrow area. All such approaches lay claim to being "a liberal education." The ultimate test, of course, is not what we teach, but what the students learn and what they become.

Thus, although the concept of a liberal education continues to reign as an article of faith that seems to unite many of us, it often masks important differences in educational philosophies, learning theories, and educational objectives. Perhaps our chief folly has been to shape our rhetoric on this issue as if there were no history of change and controversy on these issues, as if there were only one proper curriculum for everyone. There never has been a "right" curriculum, and, given rapidly changing circumstances and aspirations, the best we can hope for in the future is a continued exploration of possibilities.

The only organizing ideas that have stood steady and clear over these two millennia are that a liberal arts curriculum aims to complement the educational objectives of a narrowly technical or professional education (by imparting an understanding of our cultural inheritance, of ourselves, and of the concept of virtue, as well as of the foundations of mathematics and science) and to help create a certain type of citizen. In practice, of course, professional and liberal arts curricula overlap, and notions about the "right" type of citizen are in a constant state of flux.

Clearly, the hopes and aspirations of a liberal education always directly relate to our underlying beliefs about the nature of the human condition and of the society we wish to sustain. Indeed, to think seriously about education is to think about ideal human types for society. Educational reform, therefore, is always a kind of social protest movement. Consider, for example, some very broad historical examples.

Christian higher education in the first millennium A.D. focused on the meaning of various significant texts, principally the Bible and associated biblical commentaries. In the twelfth century, however, this tradition was challenged by the Scholastics as mere sophistry, and was replaced by a focus on logic and rationality fostered by the newly rediscovered works of Plato and Aristotle. By the fourteenth or fifteenth century, however, Scholasticism itself was replaced by what we now identify as Renaissance humanism, which shifted the focus of higher education to literary learning and rhetoric informed by Christian ethics. Medieval education (or even the education of the English Renaissance, which had a more humanistic "air") was not motivated by the pure desire to know or read the classics for their own sake, but rather by the belief that such studies would meet economic, religious, political, and other civic needs. The Renaissance version of the liberal arts was formulated and promoted as a critique of the metaphysics and natural philosophy of its day, which reformers believed avoided consideration of the true nature of the human condition. This was the humanism adopted by the American Colonial colleges, whose curriculum, therefore, focused on rhetoric, grammar, reading, memorizing, and interpreting certain "canonical" literary and theological texts that were thought to reflect and encourage the appropriate virtues. In Europe, however, the scientific revolution of the seventeenth and eighteenth centuries was already well under way, taking higher education back to something more like the Scholastic tradition, with its emphasis on logic and mathematical reasoning.

New theories and approaches to liberal education are normally motivated by positive beliefs as well as some disquiet regarding existing educational programs and the state of the human condition. If our educational curriculum requires a new sense of values, it is probably because we believe that society has the same needs. The Greeks, for example, devoted a great deal of time to understanding their new cultural/political environment and how it could be transmitted to future generations via a curriculum focused on the needed skills and virtues of the free citizen. Similarly, the founders of the Colonial colleges focused their efforts on the transmission of virtues such as temperance, justice, and courage, which would, they believed, preserve the virtues of Western civilization. Such an attitude defined a curriculum quite different from one that met the concerns of Francis Bacon, for example, for whom the objective was new knowledge and with it the power to transform and to inform.

I do not, nor should anyone else claim to have identified the most appropriate curriculum for a liberal education. Such agreement has never existed, even for brief moments in particular places. Moreover, such debates tend to focus on means rather than ends, and they miss the main points. The focus ought to be: (1) what students learn, and (2) how particular approaches serve the interests of the society we are trying to build in our age. To my mind, one can say very little about a liberal education that is timeless or fully independent of circumstance, unlike, for example, the claims of natural law. The best I can do in this respect is to try to identify some characteristics of a "liberal education" that I believe are extremely important for our time.

My own prejudices in this matter should be clear by now. I associate a liberal education in America with the particular educational needs of contemporary Western liberal democracies. Forms of a liberal education may also serve the needs of other types of societies, but I leave this matter for others to consider. Within our own society it is critical to take cognizance of two rather special characteristics. First, we should recall how atypical it is to have sustained over a number of centuries a society with a great plurality of institutions that both oppose and provide balance to the power of the state. Moreover, these institutions often are protected and financially supported by the same state. The idea that the state should support institutions that prevent its own monopoly over power and truth from becoming too extreme is, in a historical sense, quite novel.

Second, although many would claim that the historical legacy of a liberal education emphasizes our common humanity rather than the unique needs of particular individuals or groups, the contemporary development of Western liberal democracies is focused not only on the appropriate manner to ensure the rights of individuals and small family units, but also to respond to the potential need to provide constitutional space for group rights. However reasonable and important such an additional objective may be, it may make it increasingly difficult to attain the common agreements required by any coherent community. Defining individual rights within a framework in which many different kinds of groups have group rights of some sort makes it increasingly challenging, for example, to protect individual rights.

Both of these special conditions of Western liberal democracies require particular approaches to a liberal education. They include the following interdependent and overlapping needs:

1. The need (discussed later) to discover and understand the great traditions of thought that have informed the minds, hearts, and deeds of those who came before us. Whatever the distinctiveness of ourselves and our own times, we are a part of a larger—and deeper—stream of human experience. Our particular cultures may be only historical contingencies, but we ignore them at great peril to our continuing potential. Whatever the shortcomings of our predecessors—and there were many—and however limited the surviving remnants of their efforts, they remain a great source of inspiration and understanding as long as we do not deify any particular aspect of this valuable inheritance.

2. The need to free our minds and hearts from unexamined commitments (authority of all types) in order to consider new possibilities (including new "authorities") that might enhance both our own lives and, more broadly, the human condition. This corresponds with the need to build our sympathetic understanding of others who are quite different from us. In other words, we cannot allow freedom from authority to lead to excessive demands for individual gratification that are antisocial and leave no place for individual sacrifice for the common good.

3. The need to prepare all thoughtful citizens for an independent and responsible life of choice that appreciates the connectedness of things and peoples and the great uncertainty that clouds our prospects. Such citizens are able to distinguish between logical and illogical arguments, to understand the implications of the diversity we honor, and to make moral and political choices that give their individual and joint lives greater meaning. Individual responsibility and internal control are increasingly important in a world where the rigid kinship rules, strict religious precepts, and/or authoritarian rule that traditionally served to order societies have lost influence.

It also would be helpful if a liberal education encouraged and enabled students to distinguish between self-interest and community interest, between sentimentality and careful thought, and between learning and imagination, and to appreciate both the power and the limitations of knowledge. Moreover, all learning needs to be fueled by both the human imagination (e.g., what type of culture we desire) and the historically contingent characteristics of the human condition. In this latter respect, it is important at the current time to think carefully, for example, about the meaning of human existence in a world increasingly governed by technology and private markets and about the ultimate purpose of the scientific enterprise.

I recognize that these particular needs and criteria are closely related to a set of notions and institutional arrangements associated with liberal democracy. In particular, they encourage both empathetic understanding and critical assessment of the different social arrangements and cultural experiences designed to give meaning to our individual and community lives. In my view, "liberal education," like liberal politics, must be committed to tolerance and freedom. It must be committed to the acceptance of the essential ambiguities surrounding the human condition and open to the broadest stream of human ideas and experience. However, just as the radical idea of the completely neutral state is unattainable, so is a curriculum free of normative content. Just as a liberal democracy needs some notion of the good life to pursue, so a liberal education must be grounded in educational commitments and values such as tolerance and self-restraint.

In speaking either of liberal education or of liberal politics, we must also distinguish between the ideal and its actual practice in particular times and places. Despite current aspirations to openness and inclusiveness, liberal education has at times been an instrument of exclusion. The same is clearly true of liberal politics.

Finally, both liberal politics and liberal education must be tempered by the understanding that the human condition places some limit on the common agreements that can be reached by any group of citizens who have different ideas about what is most worthy, however well-meaning they are. At the end of the day, the values needed to ensure the survival of the enterprise as a whole do not allow the full expression of any and all sets of moral commitments, and some voices will inevitably feel suppressed. Liberal thought always faces tension between its commitment to tolerance and the social solidarity necessary to ensure survival of the community.

Since antiquity, citizenship has been defined by a set of rights and responsibilities that define a unique, reciprocal, and unmediated relationship between the individual and the state. The exact nature of these rights and responsibilities has, of course, changed remarkably over time, but in liberal democracies the dominant model or emphasis has been on individual rights and a sense of membership or obligation of individuals to their fellow citizens, as well as to the body politic. Somehow, despite the emphasis on the autonomy of the individual, at times the state itself is assumed to be a political and moral entity as well. Indeed, at the current time many citizens seem to achieve their sense of identity and belonging through membership in particular groups. The challenge that then arises is how to structure a liberal democracy in a manner that gives appropriate recognition, even constitutional space, to these affiliations. How, for example, would we protect those rights that arise out of the group, especially if the group has quite different ethical and cultural traditions than the polity as a whole? These issues present difficult challenges for liberal democracies, but if we did wish to incorporate multiculturalism more fully into our political life (i.e., work to eliminate the biases that favor the interests and social identities of "the" majority), our educational objectives—including what we might mean by the term *liberal education*—would change.

Despite the hopes of the Enlightenment, voluntary consent, reason, and truth have not yet completely replaced a certain amount of coercion. I have no easy answer to resolving these tensions. This is a challenge as old as the concept of democracy, and the best we can do is to continue to explore the boundaries created by the issues that separate us and respect the carefully thought-out positions of those who do not agree with us.

The curricular criteria I have suggested are interwoven with the fundamental liberal notions of the autonomy and importance of the individual. Moreover, the curricular criteria are also connected to the fundamental liberal hope of finding still better ways to both respect differences and reject domination. This, itself, is not a commitment that is shared by everyone. For me, however, it remains—together with the judicial and political system and the many civic organizations designed to give it operational meaning—the greatest guarantee of our capacity to realize and sustain meaning in our human aspirations. A liberal education, like liberal politics and unlike excessive nationalism and ethnic self-assertion, can serve what unites us rather than what divides us.

MORAL EDUCATION

From many quarters in today's society come increasingly worried expressions of concern over the lack of principled and responsible behavior in both public and private life: What has happened, people cry, to the complex web of mutual obligations and understandings that should bind us together as a community? The sources of this concern are only too easy to identify. For example, within academic communities, students, faculty, and administrators do not always exhibit a shared commitment to the values that sustain and enrich a community of learning, including honesty, nonviolence, disinterestedness, and the maintenance of thoughtful communication despite disagreements. Moreover, as the boundaries that identify different institutions and their roles and responsibilities become increasingly blurred, many find themselves unable even to identify their conflicts of interest and commitment. In a pluralistic world where no one set of values maintains a privileged position, there will always be questions about whose moral values should dominate in a particular situation, or just how we should take account of the various interests and commitments of "others." This negotiation lies at the heart of our ability to live together. Some of the questions it poses for universities are: What place should moral education occupy in the university curriculum? What are the underlying principles and rules of conduct that enable a university to meet its social responsibilities in an ethical manner?

The level of anxiety about the nature and role of moral education in the higher education curriculum has been constant ever since the founding of the American republic. Over time educators have struggled with how to balance the tensions between biblical faith and rationalism, between self and community interest, and between individual liberty and communal values. At the moment, many wish to consider a new balance between our commitments to individual liberty, private property, market competition, and due process, on the one hand, and self-restraint, communal concerns, issues of social justice, and communal obligations, on the other. Many thoughtful observers are searching for ways to reemphasize the latter set of concerns in order to halt what they perceive to be the increasing fragmentation of the social order. In an era in which market forces seem more dominant than ever, we must remind ourselves that even if private property and market competition are the most efficient ways to provide for our material needs, they may or may not produce morally acceptable results. Indeed, any single source of authority, even the market, is likely to lead to some sort of moral tyranny.

In earlier times, at American colleges and universities students and faculty alike demanded that the trustees and president select a kind of moral consensus. This was reassuring for many, but provided little nourishment for the greater part of the national community that was excluded from this consensus. Although a return to the "good old days" must be avoided, they can provide us with valuable traditions and insights as we continue to address the moral issues of our own time. The university, through its behavior and its program, should continue to play a role in helping us give our lives meaning and moral significance, in helping us understand the important contemporary lessons of "the golden rule" and the moral meaning of constraints on one's individual freedom to act. It should also help to teach us to accept the inevitable anxiety that characterizes a moral and pluralistic society committed to democracy and change. Because we have chosen pluralism and representative government over other solutions, such as official moral orthodoxies or totalitarianism, we face the special challenges of any society not absolutely bound together by something akin to a dominant religion or strong kinship tradition (including political and social fragility and the excesses that freedom often brings in its wake). Faced with these challenges, the contemporary university needs to maintain a level of moral scrutiny and criticism of existing arrangements. Its role in the moral development of its students is one vehicle through which it can contribute to our national life, especially because many of its students eventually will be in a position to exercise power and influence. At the very least, the university has some role in helping students understand why evil and goodness coexist, how paying greater attention to our moral obligations may help us clarify disagreements, and even how we might avoid the unnecessary initiation of organized violence, including war.

The last few decades have seen a virtual renaissance in the area of moral philosophy. Almost all the intellectual leadership in this development has come from university faculty. It is also true, however, that although this development has greatly increased our understanding of the moral choices we make, it has done little to decrease either the number of morally contested issues in our society or the high level of moral anxiety about those issues. In part, this is because of the many new moral choices we are facing, or because we cannot agree on the relative importance of values versus rights versus utilitarian approaches, or because we have not resolved many older issues. In fact, skepticism regarding various truth claims has only increased.

Typically, contemporary universities do not directly address the moral development of their students, for a broad set of reasons. In part, they make the mistake of identifying ethics with religious views, or interpreting ethics as prohibitions on pleasurable activities, or seeing ethics as either a private matter (a particularly mistaken idea) or as a concern to be left exclusively to

103

families and other community institutions. In part, they are concerned that any organized attempt at moral education will inevitably set in motion a movement toward moral conformity and thus undermine the principles of openness, debate, and self-criticism that are at the center of the university enterprise.

We must remember, however, that the university experience of many of our nation's future leaders will influence their moral development and, thus, their ethical judgments and their behavior as leaders. Such judgments will in turn affect all aspects of both their public and private lives. We cannot escape the reality that all of us share a moral universe with those who exercise leadership and power. Surely our students should learn to appreciate that none of us can escape the anxiety of making ethical choices and judgments, that action of any kind involves an inescapable moment of judgment where we must consider ends, means, consequences, and our particular understanding of virtue. In a society as committed to personal autonomy as ours is, there cannot be any more important subject. Furthermore, although the research university's relentless and highly successful pursuit of new knowledge is a key source of its vitality and moral authority, the new discoveries also give birth to a whole new series of moral dilemmas. The university needs, therefore, to directly address its role in the moral development of its students.

In truth, whether or not the university chooses to address the issue directly, students will at the very least continue to observe the prevailing norms. They will learn when they ought to take others' interests into account and to accept some constraints on their own freedom of action primarily from observing the behavior of the institution, its faculty, and their fellow students. They will also learn a good deal about both what to believe and what they should be committed to. Within the university environment, the behavior of the administration and faculty exercise considerable power in this respect.

I believe, therefore, that it is the faculty's and the university's responsibility to do at least two things regarding students' moral development. First, they must assist their students in understanding how to think through the nature of the ethical responsibilities that issue from their membership in a moral community, and the kind of factors that must be considered in formulating an ethical plan of action. They must build an appreciation for the challenge of deciding whether to understand moral concepts as timeless and accessible to reason, or as contingent on particular histories, cultures, antecedent virtues, and traditions. Further, they should train students to be able to appreciate whether ideas regarding moral behavior should be full of content (i.e., "thick") or more modest "outlines" governing only very general behavior patterns (i.e., "thin"). There is an extensive literature on the role of ethical judgments, in both the private and the public spheres, and on the complex moral calculations required to act in an ethical manner. Special attention is given in this literature to the responsibilities of those occupying leadership positions. Ethics cannot be restricted to private life, as Machiavelli seemed to suggest at times, nor can it be restricted to the interests of the nation state, as Hobbes seemed to suggest. At the least, we can prevent ethics being dismissed as nothing more than a convenient but self-serving set of political slogans. Many observers have paid tribute to the German university of the nineteenth century as the source of inspiration for the American research university. Few recall, however, that the informing vision of the nineteenth-century German university included the cultivation of character in addition to the transmission of knowledge and skills and the development of new knowledge. In my view, a much narrower intellectualism constantly threatens to replace this more humanistic conception of the university. We can help overcome this threat by taking moral development seriously.

Second, administration and faculty must remember that their own behavior may have a significant influence on their students' moral development. Students observe how fairly they are treated and what values are reflected in the university's rules and regulations, in their administration, and in the way that the university treats its employees. Students also observe how the university relates to the community and how faithfully faculty and administrators keep their promises and defend the values of open and thoughtful debate. How tolerant are we of others' views? How thoughtful is our feedback to our students? Is this feedback an exercise in judgment and honest criticism, or is it merely punitive? Do we faculty and administrators allow our individual liberty to overwhelm all other values? Do we shock and patronize our students or awaken them? Do our programs assist students in entering the world of internal speculation and reflective thought? As students observe the behavior of the faculty, the administration, and the governing boards, they will recognize in our actions whether we are taking adequate account of the interests of others. Thoughtful observers will discern for themselves whether a university remains a symbol of enlightenment or an institution that identifies the good society with the special privileges of the status quo.

Let me suggest a number of areas in the everyday concerns of leaders of higher education where they can and should take moral leadership.

1. What set of criteria ought to qualify a candidate for admission to a particular university, and precisely whose interests do such decisions serve?

2. What ought a university teach, and precisely whose interests have been taken into account in this decision?

3. How should a university treat its students, staff, and faculty? Why should it treat them in this manner, and precisely whose interests are being served by these decisions?

4. Ought the university to focus its primary efforts on promoting intellectual virtues? And, if so, precisely whose interests are being served by this decision?

5. Ought the university to continue to prefer moral anxiety over moral conformity? Why should it do so, and precisely whose interests are being taken into account in reaching this decision?

6. Should the university support "good works," why should it do this, and precisely whose interests are being served?

7. What rules, if any, should characterize membership in the academic community, what is the rationale for these decisions, and precisely whose interests are being served?

8. What is the role of authority in a university? Who gets to decide this, and precisely who is served by the result?

9. Regarding faculty work effort, what is the balance between internal and external commitments, and between teaching and research, and precisely whose interests are best served by these decisions?

There are many potential additions to this illustrative list. The important point is that leaders in higher education can simultaneously exert moral and intellectual leadership by articulating why universities make the choices they do and precisely whose interests these choices are designed to serve.

In this context, I cannot avoid the question: What role should moral education have in the curriculum itself? The issue evokes both disagreement and great uneasiness. The greatest source of uneasiness stems from the fear of being perceived as establishing some kind of moral orthodoxy. Many feel it is no longer appropriate for the institution to decide what ethics or whose ethics ought to be taught. Although legitimate, this concern should not prevent us from addressing the issue directly. Why should our curriculum not offer students an opportunity to develop their capacities to identify and analyze ethical issues? Uncertainty on issues does not prevent teaching about them. All that is needed is to propose the careful evaluation of alternatives. The discussion of moral issues is important even if we do not have a "ready" answer. Clearly, complex moral reasoning is not a substitute for moral behavior, yet it is a necessary beginning. If we unite this capacity with an understanding of the deep moral ambiguity of many situations and an ongoing commitment to democracy and concern for others, we will have accomplished a great deal. Most of all, we can hope to help our students to respect and support those public figures who seriously address our obligations to promote peace, justice, and freedom, both at home and abroad, instead of accusing them of being "moralizers" who are too eager to sacrifice our national "interests." I feel strongly that it is time to move our society away from being full of excuses and short of shame!

Because I am a professor of economics and public affairs, I would like to give some practical examples of how the analysis of public policy issues often addressed in the curriculum can be used to identify and clarify ethical issues. The examples I use involve economic inequality and globalization.

Inequality

There has been a great deal of discussion in recent years regarding the meaning and consequences of the growing inequality in income and wealth in the United States. The basic facts, which are not in dispute, are startling:

1. Over the last three decades, there has been virtually no change in the inflation-adjusted hourly wages paid to the bottom half of all wage earners, despite some transitory movements up and down.

2. In recent decades, the family incomes of poor people have risen much more slowly than the family incomes of others. Indeed, the richer the family, the faster the rate of income growth. This pattern contrasts sharply with the decades immediately following World War II, when the financial growth of low-income families was faster.

3. Compared to other advanced industrialized countries, we not only seem to have become more polarized in terms of income, wealth, and education, but *may* have a lower level of intergenerational mobility with regard to these factors.

My question: Should such facts command the attention of citizens and public policy makers? I think so, for a number of reasons. First, we should constantly inquire whether the existing distribution of income, wealth, and education, and, in particular, the welfare and fate of lower-income families and individuals are consistent with our sense of social justice. Second, we need to understand the social, political, and economic implications of such a state of affairs, as well as the implications, if any, for public policy. This much is straightforward, but as we begin to think thoughtfully about these matters, a number of difficulties arise. First, there are competing standards regarding how we should judge the morally justified distribution of benefits and burdens in a particular society. For example, should benefits and burdens be distributed equally, by demonstrated need, by merit, by the operation of private markets, or by some utilitarian calculation? Second, we know that however defined, income and wealth inequality has both negative and positive characteristics. On the positive side, financial inequality *may* encourage high levels of human capital, savings, investment, and innovation, which could make all members of society better off. On the negative side, incomes may have been allocated unjustly because of discrimination, the ethically unjustified accumulation of productive assets in certain hands, or other factors. In any event, certain levels of inequality may lead to a wide variety of antisocial behaviors and a loss of the social solidarity necessary for any well-functioning society.

The appropriate response of public policy depends on two challenging considerations: our sense of what social justice requires, and a set of beliefs regarding the empirical state of the world. Yet in both these crucial arenas, uncertainty and ambiguity reign. Different theories of social justice yield different ideas regarding the most just distribution of resources. Moreover, these alternative theories exist in a kind of philosophical equipoise, with none dominating all others. In addition, empirical assessments differ widely regarding the economic impact of, for example, any new public policy initiatives to transfer income from high-to-low-income families. Thus, while some see President Bush's tax proposals as yet another unearned dividend to the rich and undeserving, others see them as part of a strategy to make *everyone* better off.

However strongly we may feel about these issues, we all must acknowledge the uncertainty not only regarding the optimal balance among freedom, justice, and efficiency, but also about which is the most practical path to take us to that target. The growing gap between rich and poor in our country offends my sense of social justice and, I believe, generates negative side effects for us all. I believe that something significant should be done soon to remedy the situation. Nevertheless, I must also acknowledge that the situation is complex both empirically and as a matter of social justice, and I must be prepared to adjust my opinions if contrary evidence accumulates. Moreover, policy makers have also to confront the matter of intergenerational equality, which focuses on the appropriate allocation or reallocation of our national income. I leave the discussion of this matter to another occasion.

For those with the responsibility for actually choosing a course of action in this arena, there is no avoiding the anguish involved in trying to create a better world. For students to leave the university without the understanding that most decisions, in private or public life, are bathed in ambiguity and uncertainty is for them to leave unprepared for leadership in their families, their professions, their communities, and in our liberal democracy. I will turn now to my second example, regarding the implications of globalization.

Globalization

Globalization is not simply a matter of economics. Its full meaning reaches far beyond matters of international trade, comparative advantage, and exchange rates. The phenomenon of globalization clearly expands, for example, the issue of income inequality. Globalization, blurring the boundaries between domestic and international economic and political polices, raises directly the great question of what new political and constitutional arrangements need to be set up in order to promote peace, justice, pluralism, and freedom in our newly interdependent world. Moreover, the nature of present day globalization causes events and conditions at a distance from us to feel close. Globalization is important even as a public health matter, because it has long been observed that disease follows the movement of goods, services, and people across the globe.

Globalization has set loose a wide variety of forces that will not only precipitate important institutional change in many societies, but will also cause our various national arrangements to become more alike. Thus globalization will have significant impacts not only on a wide variety of political, cultural, and social institutions, but also on the human narratives that societies have developed to give their community lives some transcendental meaning. The era of globalization therefore presents us with a new set of ethical challenges.

Dealing with these new challenges requires a much improved knowledge of the empirical state of the world. Let me be more specific. For much of human history, communities occupying different spots on Earth could almost be considered as living in different worlds. Their informing narratives needed to have little relationship to or acknowledgment of one another. Different languages, cultures, and traditions developed, including different understandings of the obligations or ethical responsibilities we have to one another. For most purposes the activities of one community had little or no impact on other communities. Since the age of exploration, and especially in recent decades, this situation has permanently changed. Growing environmental problems, newly interdependent economies, and, to a lesser extent, newly instituted common laws and the slow collapse of the distinction between international and domestic conflicts are all evidence of this widespread shift. Today we must assume that many of our actions have significant impacts on other communities. Today as never before we are bound together in a vastly enlarged moral community composed of groups with a wide variety of traditions and different views regarding substantive moral issues. In this new environment we are forced, even if only super-

111

ficially, to consider, or reconsider, the level of ethical priority we give to the interests of our own citizens.

Very early on, humans must learn to distinguish between their primary caregivers and all others. The very nature of the human condition means that young people spend a considerable length of time fully dependent on their primary caregivers. This means that they must learn not only to distinguish between their caregivers and others, but also to develop a preference for these caregivers. This necessary preference of young children for their primary caregivers nevertheless creates an obstacle to the early development of a wider circle of trust even within a given cultural tradition and certainly beyond that tradition. Slowly this circle of mutually empathetic support and preference may expand, but it tends to do so slowly and incompletely. How do we then meet the challenge of sustaining a national or even an international community in which many traditions must assume greater obligations to one another? When imagining the nature and structure of ethical systems designed to bring together a wide variety of ethical traditions into a common moral community, it may prove easier to define a list of mutual rights and obligations than to agree on a common set of underlying principles. This "easier" task would already be a substantial accomplishment, although the lack of underlying principles would make it very difficult, perhaps impossible, to deal with the matters of interpretation that would inevitably arise. A further challenge will be deciding on acceptable strategies to safeguard rights and implement obligations.

This situation presents a new and difficult challenge for international justice, one that we have yet to resolve even within pluralistic states, namely, how to honor various group traditions in a context that preserves certain group rights while ensuring that everyone's individual rights are respected.

Finally, the seemingly inexorable increase in the "thickness" of globalization requires us to examine anew the claim that a universal ethical code can be found and eventually adopted by everyone. In fact, we now need to address questions such as:

How far can or should globalization proceed in the context of different moral visions each informed by its own cultural and historical context? Are there some limited number of moral commitments that we all can share, and if so, which are they? Can we all adopt the same type of moral reasoning? These and similar questions have not yet been answered, but they represent exciting challenges for all of us. A great deal is at stake. My somewhat utopian hope is that the age of globalization may be the moment in human history when rights, interests, and utilitarian calculations converge to yield a clearer moral landscape for us all.

PROFESSIONAL EDUCATION

Throughout much of the history of higher education, professional schools and their faculties dominated the university. This is no longer the case. Indeed, I want to consider the following questions: Does professional education stand on the periphery of the "real university"? How does a liberal arts education relate to a professional education? My two conclusions: Professional education does not now and never did stand on the periphery of the university, and the basic aims of professional education are startlingly similar to the aims of a liberal arts education. Indeed, the most valuable part of education for any learned profession is that aspect that teaches future professionals to think, read, compare, discriminate, analyze, form judgments, and generally enhance their mental capacity to confront the ambiguities and enigmas of the human condition. After all, a learned profession is in part a mode of cultural explanation and social understanding. Given my conclusions, I call for a closer partnership between the faculties of professional schools and the faculties of the arts and sciences.

I would like to begin by asking, in a rather rhetorical fashion, a provocative question, and then provide what some may consider equally provocative answers. My question is: Why are the faculties of so many professional schools, particularly those at research universities, anxious or uneasy about their status within the university? Another way of posing this question is: Why have the arts and sciences faculties come to believe that they are the sole definers and defenders of the soul of the university? Adopting such an attitude is possible only when one exaggerates the differences between a liberal education on the one hand and professional education on the other, or consciously or unconsciously pits them against each other. This rivalry may be a historical legacy of the fact that throughout most of the history of higher education, the professional faculties dominated the university. Only over the last century or so has the influence of the arts and science faculties grown and been productive, though in truth this influence is somewhat exaggerated.

Interestingly, among the four faculties of the medieval university, *Philosophia* (arts and sciences) was the poor sister of theology, medicine, and law. Indeed, preparation for the learned professions of law, theology, and medicine was the primary raison d'être of both the medieval and the Colonial university. Moreover, as I have already noted, higher education in America began quite clearly as professional education. How do we square this history with the widespread myth that the liberal arts alone occupy the moral high ground of the university and that the arts and sciences faculty must serve as the guardian of the university's soul? This distorted image of both the history and the current reality of higher education needs to be put aside before it hinders the ongoing vitality of the entire enterprise.

Let me return, however, to the issue of why some professional schools are uneasy about their role within the university. Is it that:

1. They are anxious because Thorstein Veblen suggested that law schools had as much reason to be part of the university as dancing schools? If ancient and learned professions such as law occupy an uneasy seat, no wonder the other professional schools are anxious! On the other hand, it is hard to know whether some of Veblen's best-known assertions are meant as social criticism or social satire!

114

2. They are uneasy because their professional and/or scholarly claims are tenuous, or because they cannot fully establish the validity of requiring a certain knowledge and skill base before allowing entrance to the profession?

3. They are anxious because they are not sure of their professions' prerogatives to judge one another's mistakes, to charge fees independent of outcomes, and to control state licensing? Their colleagues in the arts and sciences probably share this particular anxiety.

4. They are anxious because they believe that they are indeed at the periphery of the institution, particularly if they do not teach undergraduates?

5. They are uneasy because universities in the English-speaking world remain in the thrall of Cardinal Newman's (1999, p. 51) assertion that "a university after all should be formally based and live in the faculty of Arts . . . "? He only grudgingly added ". . . with a reasonable association with the learned professions of law, medicine and theology."

I believe that Cardinal Newman had it quite wrong, both as regards society's aspirations for the university and as a matter of the actual historical record. I prefer Alfred North Whitehead's (1929, p. 139) view of the university: "The justification for a university is that it preserves the connection between knowledge and the zest for life [i.e., via the necessary movement of questions, ideas, and scholarship between professional schools and center of research and teaching in the arts and sciences] and by involving the young and the old in the imaginative [i.e., speculative and reflective] consideration of learning." In a similar vein, one might recall the thoughtful remark of W.E.B. DuBois (1903, p. 84): "Education . . . [is] that organ of fine adjustment between real life and the growing knowledge of life."

Although American universities have been shaped by rival beliefs about the ends they should serve—scholarship, virtue, or practical service to society—they seem to share a common set of bureaucratic or managerial categories. In some respects these

115

categories themselves have had deleterious effects. For example, the establishment of distinct faculties in the professional schools and, at times, in graduate and undergraduate education often serves not only to erase some of the communal character of the university, but also to hide many of the common aims of liberal and professional education. Equally important, such separations forfeit the new ideas and solutions to old problems that only closer cooperation can provide. Indeed, few imperatives are now more essential to the future vitality of a distinguished university than improving our communication across existing bureaucratic lines. In my judgment, the rigid separation of professional from undergraduate and graduate education within the same institution (an American innovation) is a serious bureaucratic error. Yet by now it has become almost deified by a mistaken educational ideology. We should put aside the issue of whether or not to mix the so-called professional and academic, and focus intently on the most effective way of doing so.

At least we are fortunate that the initial design of the American research university kept undergraduate, graduate, and professional education in the same institutions; we thus retain an exciting, if unfulfilled, potential—one of the great "hidden" and unexploited aspects of the American research university.

IN PLACE OF A CONCLUSION

It is too soon to grasp the full meaning of the many astonishing developments with which the last decades of the twentieth century ended. The startling political transformation of Eastern Europe and the former Soviet Union—and perhaps China—is but one example. Others are the internationalization of the world's economies, the growth of population, the movement of peoples at unprecedented levels, and the establishment of worldwide information networks. Indeed, the twentieth century opened with the rediscovery of Mendel's paper on genetics and heredity and closed with the completion and publication of the map of the human genome. One way or another, there seems little question that a new global transformation of some sort is now under way. These astonishing events, and others, have caused us to begin rethinking existing ideas and commitments across an ideological spectrum that runs from the bases of national polities to the possibilities of empire, from national security arrangements to the future role of tribal solidarity in international affairs, from the continuing viability of the idea of a nation to the meaning of socialism in an increasingly internationalized (transgovernment) economy and from the meaning of individual freedoms to the bases of the moral commitments that create coherent communities.

In America, for example, many are concerned that our social arrangements have resulted in too many Americans feeling disconnected from the country's future. Some thoughtful observers believe that our current policies, political arrangements, and social structure may not provide the cultural assets necessary for our continued cultural and economic vitality. At the very least, we seem in need of a revitalized set of mobilizing beliefs, commitments, and imagined objectives capable of fueling both individual and national effort.

Recent events have led many to feel that our society is not really as open and equitable either as we believe or as it ought to be. This demands, therefore, a more critical look at the moral and political parameters of our traditions and institutions and the arrangements that distribute power and other benefits. If we needed any further evidence of the need for renewed thinking in these areas, consider that liberal democratic values are being criticized for putting both too much *and* too little stress on the role of individual rights over against the claims of tradition, social stability, and community. Symbolic of these uncertainties is the fact that in America, the equal protection clause of our Constitution is now invoked to confer rights on virtually all persons who believe themselves excluded from certain benefits under existing arrangements. Even the concept of diaspora, formerly connoting the despised, displaced, and disenfranchised, now rises

117

from the ashes of history to present "imagined homelands" as a cultural ideal in an increasingly pluralistic world.

This general ferment bespeaks the search for a meaningful set of centering values and will certainly have implications for higher education, as do the ongoing changes in demographics, the nature and distribution of work, and attitudes toward government expenditures and taxes.

With respect to our teaching programs, many believe that we have become not only too "scattered" and specialized, but also too removed from the overall development of students and not fully responsive to their changing educational needs. Yet others believe the opposite: that our teaching is not deep or demanding enough and that we pay too much attention to students' developmental and social needs.

All in all, the Western university has been a remarkably durable and adaptive institution. Although always the focus of criticism and some disappointment, these institutions continue to be valued by Western societies, sometimes as society's best hope for change, sometimes for reassurance about traditional moral commitments. Notwithstanding the many revolutions that seem to characterize contemporary life—the burgeoning of telecommunications, the development of a so-called politics of difference; the transformation of the nation state; the redistribution of people, capital, production facilities, and products around the globe; and the perceived diminution of moral certainties—it is unlikely that evolving events will bring about the demise of universities as we know them.

Despite their many shortfalls, despite changing demographics, expectations, and public and private priorities, despite a somewhat deteriorating physical infrastructure, and despite a sometimes shaken faith (both internal and external) in their potential civic contribution, these institutions will, I believe, once again prove capable of adapting in a manner that reflects an understanding of the current environment. There are few institutions with such continuing potential as universities to deliver new social dividends to society; therefore there is little reason to put them on the endangered species list. Universities may have to do with less; they will certainly have to conduct a searching reexamination of their programs in the light of contemporary realities. But I believe that their unique potential for learning, which centers around the power of the person-to-person encounter, their demonstrated capacity for largely peaceful interaction across many cultural divides, and their continuing ability to challenge the familiar, will make them indispensable assets for the future now unfolding.

Some Ethical Dimensions
of Scientific Progress

Science has become a defining activity within our society. For some, scientific progress has even come to be an integral part of a new faith. This new faith is based on the belief that human progress in all spheres will be promoted, in some unspecified and mysterious way, by advances on the scientific frontier. For these "believers," what was once a faith in the divine unfolding of history and/or salvation has been replaced by a faith in the capacity of scientific progress to find a better balance among ultimate objectives such as justice, equality, excellence, autonomy, social cohesion, and peace. In this essay I address a more modest topic, namely, the underlying characteristics of a particular set of ethical challenges and tensions that always accompany forward movement of the scientific frontier. Since time immemorial, human communities have been actors in a drama surrounding new technologies and their impact on the human condition, a drama that reflects an underlying tension between *what is* (which seems "natural") and *what we are about to create* (which seems "unnatural," optional, or artificial). This drama requires the attention of public policy makers and the nation's research universities because both communities have become central actors in the nation's scientific enterprise.

There are two special reasons why these matters are of special interest to the nation's academic community. First, the ethical issues bring together the world of science with the world of meaning and our understanding of the nature of the human condition. They require serious conversations between scientists and others, discussions that need to be informed by the intellectual resources and apparatus of the social sciences and humanities. Our society offers no better venue for such conversations than our university campuses. Moreover, I believe the increasing importance of these matters now makes it imperative that they have an effect on the teaching agenda of all institutions committed to liberal learning. Indeed, they could serve to bridge the considerable gap that still divides the sciences, the social sciences, and the humanities.

Second, the ethical issues I will address arise directly from the unprecedented success of the scientific enterprise, an arena in which the nation's research universities play an increasingly central role. Indeed, the faculties of the nation's research universities not only are one of the primary vehicles for the execution of publicly sponsored research, but they also greatly influence the nation's science policies, the scientific agenda itself, the broad nature of the public's research priorities, and the public's understanding of how new knowledge will be deployed. Faculty, therefore, have a special responsibility to participate in the inevitable discourse that will arise on how to give our new knowledge its moral resonance and greatest meaning. Although I will focus a great deal on biomedical science, much of what I have to say applies to the entire scientific frontier.

In addition to scientific norms such as truth telling, attribution, peer review, and other standards of practice designed to avoid error and self-deception on the one hand and to foster the growth of knowledge on the other, ethics more broadly conceived and public policy have a significant influence on the very character of the scientific enterprise. Scientists have values and duties qua scientists. Science itself is a collective human endeavor shaped by considerations both internal and external. We only have to consider matters such as patents, immigration rules, trade policies, regulations of various stripes, education and research subsidies, and government laboratories to remind ourselves of the pervasive influence of public policy on the nature and scope of the nation's scientific enterprise.

Moreover, science is not an independent practice unconnected to society's larger cultural goals. Scholarship is seldom produced as an end in itself. Although science is intimately tied to the values, laws, incentives, and aspirations of the social, cultural, po-

121

litical, and economic environment, it also can be a somewhat independent agent of change and progress. Its agenda, however, is determined, in large part, by the preoccupations of the time. Science is not an enterprise that is self-sufficient or capable either of fully endowing our lives with meaning or connecting us to some grander scheme of things. In particular, standards for judging the nature of our mutual obligations to one another, or the constraints on our individual freedom we ought to accept in the interests of other moral agents cannot be provided by science. Although science has no tools for deciding whether a particular act is ethical or not, the ethical issues arising from various scientific developments will influence the shape of the evolving scientific agenda. The particular ethical problems that I will consider focus not on the ethical lapses of individual scientists or research groups, or the ethical norms of scientific research, but on the much more prevalent and fundamental ethical issues that arise precisely because the scientific frontier is moving forward.

Although I consider myself a scholar, I am not a scientist in the normal meaning of that term. I must say, however, that there have been many moments when I have wished I were a scientist, because it must be very satisfying to be part of one of the greatest and most creative human activities ever. The scientific enterprise enables us to understand better the human condition, to comprehend more fully the natural world and, therefore, to deal more effectively with the contingencies of human existence. Indeed, the scientific method not only is one of the most powerful intellectual ideas ever developed, but also provides an extraordinary framework for understanding the natural world and our place in it. Moreover, because a great deal of science addresses the needs and hopes of so many people, it is full of ethical significance and meaning. Indeed, science, scientists, and their supporters are part of a great humanitarian enterprise aimed at the relief of suffering, the enhancement of the human condition, and the achievement of a better understanding of ourselves and the natural world. The work of scientists has dramatically altered the type of society we live in and has given new direction and understanding to the idea of progress. It has encouraged us, for good or ill, to deepen our belief in humankind's capacity to control nature and shape our own destiny. Thus it has changed our ideas regarding humankind's place in the universe, our relationship to other forms of life, the interaction of the sacred and secular, and the relationship between natural and cultural forces.

Science is a magnificent achievement of the human mind, and the manner in which scientists order the facts of the natural world is often full of subtlety and beauty. As a cultural activity, science can also be a great source of hope for humankind. It is not enough, however, to be in awe of science. It is critical to understand both its promises and its limitations. Both scientists and nonscientists need to understand that science is not some vast impersonal force unconnected to society's other major concerns. Such thinking not only is a serious error, but also would induce in nonscientists a sense of fear rather than of beneficence and opportunity. This would not serve anyone's interests.

Although the cumulative accomplishments of science can hardly be overstated, we must acknowledge that they necessarily bring in their wake a series of problematic issues. It is doubtful, for example, that more science always leads to more social dividends, that the scientific agenda is always focused on the most important issues, that the norms of science are adequate to ensure public accountability, that the promise of science is always fulfilled, that science can take the measure of all things, or that new knowledge is neutral in its moral and practical consequences. Science is a social activity. Scientific activities cannot benefit everyone's interests at the same time, and they are inevitably influenced by ideologies and conflicts of interest. Indeed, some have gone so far as to suggest that science, like other activities and policies, simply serves those who profit from the existing social order.

From my perspective, the important point to remember is that scientists and nonscientists alike are part of a common moral community, bound to one another by a shared vision of the kind of society we would like to become, by various mechanisms of

123

priority setting and accountability, and by the nature of the obligations we have to the interests of others. These ties create and sustain a wider civil community. Thus, in a scientific age such as our own, serious conversations and social negotiations between scientists and nonscientists on matters of mutual concern are both extremely important and ethically significant.

Just as there are those who thought that the use of new technology to enhance human capacities and traits was likely to improve the human condition, there have always been others who had much more ambivalent attitudes. They worried, for example, that the deployment of new technologies would make it more difficult to articulate certain boundary lines, such as that between the sacred and the secular, or that between human and nonhuman animals. There are, of course, many ways of being human, but the development of new human powers at any moment in time requires some redrawing of the demarcation points that define human aspirations and responsibilities. Thus, when the world of natural theology, with its notion that God had formed the world just as it exists, gave way to the natural sciences, with its notion that humans were not outside and above nature but intimately related to all of life, we had to undergo a shift in our conception of what it means to be human. Likewise today many feel that the extraordinary success of the scientific enterprise is once again making it more difficult to understand what it means to be human, to comprehend the nature of our new opportunities and responsibilities, and, therefore, to articulate the nature of our moral obligations to one another. Thus, science and scientists create ethical challenges—not because of their occasional ethical lapses, but because of their accomplishments. Indeed, the very success of the contemporary scientific enterprise ensures the continuous flow of new anxieties and a variety of new ethical challenges. The question is: Do we have adequate moral resources to understand how we should deploy and/or constrain humankind's ever-growing capacity to "master" not only our environment, but also the nature of who we are and what our descendants will become? Should our rapidly growing knowledge base encourage us to think of human beings as the ultimate authors of our own destiny, and, therefore, to take full responsibility for all that develops? The extraordinary accomplishments of science and technology both elevate and oppress us, haunt and encourage us, fill us with hope and dread.

My interest in these issues stems from the common observation that the pace and complexity of the transformations resulting from new scientific discoveries and the deployment of new technologies are making our time uniquely unstable and uncertain. Indeed, it seems that these developments require us constantly to reinvent ourselves, challenging our ability to sustain a sense of continuity or identity.

Thus, although I am not a scientist, I care about scientists' interests and I hope and expect that they will care about mine. Moreover, I am one of those nonscientists who has had a sustained interest in the intersection of science and public policy, and a special interest in those issues where scientific developments generate a good deal of unease and moral anxiety. I have had to deal with such challenges as a university president and faculty member with a long-term interest in the responsibilities of the American research university. Finally, I became even more stimulated by and committed to these concerns during the period from 1996 to 2001, when I served as chair of the National Bioethics Advisory Commission. During that time I was surprised by the level of unease occasioned by scientific advances. Specifically, shortly after the commission was formed by President Clinton, I found myself trying to understand the near panic, even among some scientists, that followed the 1997 publication of the "Dolly" experiment, which demonstrated science's capacity to clone a mammal. The somatic cell nuclear transfer techniques utilized the genetic material of only one parent, yet it led to the development of a mature adult. Among other things, this accomplishment reminded us that each of our cells contains all of our DNA and implied that eventually it might be possible for any of us to create a "delayed" genetic twin of ourselves.

125

The "sudden" prospect of being able to clone human beings brought on what could be termed general hysteria. Fortunately, it was short-lived. In this context, it is interesting to recall that one of the chief claims of the medieval alchemists of the fourteenth and fifteenth centuries, in addition to their ability to create gold from base metals, was their capacity to create minute human beings by artificial means. Indeed, in the early sixteenth century, Paracelsus claimed to have a precise formula for the physical generation of a person from a mixture of semen and blood without the need for female participation in the process. There seems to be a certain kind of poetic justice in the contrasting "Dolly technique," which requires no male participation—only a cell, an ovum, and a female's womb.

In 1997 it became clear that the emotionally charged reaction to the Dolly experiment had been conditioned more by images from works of science fiction, current and ancient, and by some imaginative film and video productions, as well as by a certain amount of pent-up concern regarding the ultimate meaning of contemporary scientific developments, than by any understanding of the promise and limitations of the particular science involved in "Dolly-type" cloning. Perhaps the most influential of all the works of science fiction in this area was Mary Shelley's *Frankenstein*, which she wrote as a teenager in 1816. It focused on a scientist who was destroyed by the person, or monster, he had created. *Frankenstein* raised the question of whether science would refashion our world or destroy it. Almost a century later, in 1896, H. G. Wells in *The Island of Doctor Moreau* characterized the painful and death-defying attempt by a scientist to attain mastery over evolution. More recently, in Michel Houellebecq's *Elementary Particles* (2000), a renowned geneticist tries to define a new genetic science that will abolish from the human psyche both love and pain (because the former causes the latter), and thus permit the construction of a post-human person. Even more sobering are our only too real and too recent memories, not only of the organized state-sponsored efforts to create a

126

master race by the Nazis, but also of the misguided efforts here and abroad to introduce various eugenic schemes to shape the gene pool of the next generation. In retrospect, these programs were based on naive science and the even more naive notion that we could find a purely technical solution to an array of perceived social problems. Little wonder, then, that the Dolly experiment met with by such widespread consternation.

Even after the initial fears subsided, however, the underlying concern continued about what effect human reproductive cloning (using the "Dolly" technique) would have on the human narrative in general and in particular on the formation of our identity and our sense of self-worth. The critics deployed arresting phrases such as "playing God," "the inviolability and dignity of each person," and the "unnatural" nature of the new enterprises, all suggesting that these events were presenting dire challenges to our preferred concepts of human nature and our favored structures of human societies.

The repeated use of the notion that "Dolly-type" cloning somehow violated our human nature raised my own unease, because in my view there are many human natures, each of these evolves over time, and no one particular notion of human nature has sole possession of the moral high ground. To my mind, the notion of a unique human nature is usually brought forward by those trying to defend a particular way of being human or a particular set of values and/or virtues. At least since Aristotle, there have been thoughtful attempts to articulate the specific differences between humans and nonhuman animals. Moreover, at least since the fifteenth century, many have focused on the unique capacity of humans to reshape themselves in significant ways. Thus, if the term *human nature* has any well-defined meaning, it is that of a manifold and evolving existence shaped, in part, by human choices. Even if we all agreed precisely on what it meant, it should not be cloaked in an aura of immutability and even sanctity. Even Rousseau, who worried a great deal about humankind's increasing distance from nature, understood

127

that this development resulted from human beings making choices in the pursuit of what Rousseau considered the folly of perfectibility. Finally, it became clear to me that the controversies surrounding reproductive cloning and, later, human embryonic stem cell research were examples of distress over a much wider area of current scientific and clinical endeavor in a field that could be characterized as assisted reproductive technologies and genetic engineering.

Some critics were concerned that the constant pursuit of new technologies represents a misuse of social resources and is likely to result in a widening gap between rich and poor. Other critics suggested that the use of these technologies was an act of hubris, in which humankind assumed too much power and responsibility. Perhaps it was dangerous for humans always to yearn for more knowledge and a deeper understanding of the underlying mysteries of our finite existence and the nature of eternity. It is often suggested, for example, that it would be better to take our chances in the genetic lottery than look for more controllable methods of reproduction through new technologies such as preimplantation genetic screening, genetic engineering, or even reproductive cloning. This attitude raises the benefits of uncertainty to new levels! If we took this particular argument to its logical limit, we should be investigating ways to induce even more chance into the reproductive process and into human affairs in general.

Many of the ethical issues raised by contemporary, scientific, and technological progress have been with us for a very long time. Yet suddenly there arose an unusual chorus of demands for oversight and restriction on scientific work itself, especially publicly sponsored research. Thoughtful citizens were and are talking of specific measures to constrain—even criminalize—the conduct of scientists and the behavior of other social agencies. In the midst of this swelling chorus, I ask myself whether there is anything novel in the ethical issues and anxieties swirling around contemporary developments on the scientific frontier. Have the

128

cumulative effect of the many startling successes generated by the ideas of the Enlightenment—with its emphases on scientific progress, individual freedom, and cultural pluralism—reached a point where we can no longer articulate the necessary conditions for human flourishing? Have the Enlightenment virtues of rationality, autonomy, discipline, and accumulation been unexpectedly transformed into a highly developed culture of materialistic narcissism? Do we simply lack the moral resources to deal with the full implications of current developments on the scientific frontier and what seems like the incipient erosion of established or traditional norms? Or are we simply witnessing the normal difficulty of adapting our lives to new circumstances? Do recent developments on the scientific frontier in fact present us with any really new ethical issues?

WHAT'S REALLY NEW

In its most general form, characterizations of scientific progress as enigmatic and ambiguous in meaning are as old as the written record of Western civilization. On the other hand, there are quite new dimensions to the issue, some of which are especially relevant to individuals and institutions that consider themselves part of the scientific and broader scholarly enterprise. As I began thinking about these issues, I quickly came to two conclusions.

First, attributing feelings of unease and even moral outrage regarding developments on the scientific frontier solely to ignorance or selfishness, or to "Luddites," is both an intellectual error and a policy mistake that serves no one. There may be those who, as Carl Sagan is reputed to have said, think with their gut and wish that emotion could replace arguments. Still, human history tells us that we need to take the trouble to understand the serious and thoughtful concerns behind such reactions.

Second, the nature of current and prospective developments in human genetics, not to mention other sciences, requires us to rethink or at least revisit some of our basic concepts of moral and social philosophy. For example, it raises with greater urgency questions such as:

1. Should the well-being of future generations be more (or less) present in our moral calculations, given our new capacity to exert greater control over their genetic inheritance?

2. If our genetic endowment proves to have a strong impact on our behavior, do we need to rethink our notions of human freedom, human equality, human identity, human responsibility, and even the social organization of society?

3. What should reproductive freedom mean in the context of the "new" genetics and associated techniques in assisted reproductive technologies?

4. What moral limits, if any, should there be to human activity and human responsibility?

5. Can we any longer maintain a wide and clear scientific and/ or spiritual boundary between humans and other animals?

6. Have these new technologies expanded the range of things of which we ought to seek a just distribution? What could we possibly mean, for example, by an equitable distribution of genes?

7. If genetic engineering becomes a clinical modality, do we have any obligation to use this technology to equalize social or economic opportunity?

8. Is technology finally going to overwhelm us rather than serve us?

Although a whole range of longstanding human social practices influence the genomes of our children, these new scientific and technological developments may give us substantially increased power to "design" the genomes of future generations. This new "power" requires us to review public, institutional, and professional policies that regulate how we deploy it. At the very least, therefore, these prospective new biomedical interventions require us to revisit certain central issues in moral philosophy that focus on the question of what it now means to be human and whether or not this requires us to restrict, for example, the way we deploy our developing knowledge in human genetics. Although such a dramatic change on the scientific frontier is not unprecedented, as Copernicus and Galileo could certainly testify, contemporary developments are unique in the sense that they must be incorporated into a society and culture that is already characterized by an unprecedented amount of novelty.

Perhaps the best-known image on the ceiling of the Vatican's Sistine Chapel is that of a force beyond human understanding and responsibility (in this case, God) reaching out to create humankind (in the form of Adam). The basic idea that there are issues beyond human understanding has been central to the creation myths or traditional narratives of all societies. Moreover, what some have called the Genesis problem, or how to decide the genetic makeup of future generations, has been a matter decided primarily by chance or other nonhuman forces. With the dawn of the genetic age, however, we are about to gain the capacity to extend our control over future generations in a radically new way. Does this prospective new ability to manipulate our own nature alter our view of the sacred and the ultimate meaning of being human? It certainly alters the spectrum of human possibilities and responsibilities that now confront us. In this heady environment, it seems to some that we are about to cross a dangerous moral threshold. To others, however, human nature has always been an evolving concept or set of concepts, at least partly formed by human choice and action. Is the advance of science to be thought of as an attempt to undermine God's authority and plan, or as a celebration of the tools we have developed (or have been given by God) to overcome perceived obstacles to human flourishing?

The dawn of this new genetic age is a source of great hope for some and great dread for others. Is the future the carrier of new hopes for the greater realization of our humanity, or the carrier of new fears? For some, new knowledge deepens a defining aspect of our humanity, namely, the ability to control our environment. Others see this knowledge as a threat to those aspects of the human condition that they feel is most precious and most in need of preservation. Other contemporary scientific develop-

131

ments, such as those in physics and astrophysics, raise analogous issues regarding the origin of the universe, the origin of life itself, and the origin of the human mind. For example, it is still difficult for most people to "believe" that the chemical constituents of everything on Earth were cooked up in some distant star about five billion years ago, considerably after the birth of the universe!

In trying to build my own understanding of the anxieties and ethical tensions raised by recent scientific developments, I have found it useful to think of the collection of issues as consisting of three distinct components:

1. A very old, even ancient, dimension;

2. A relatively new aspect that arises in the special context of liberal democracies;

3. A very new aspect that arises because of particular developments all along the scientific frontier. In this essay, however, I will confine my attention to current developments on the biomedical frontier.

I would like to deal with each of these components in turn: from the old problem, to the relatively new problem, to the very new problem. I will proceed, therefore, in a kind of chronological order.

THE OLD, EVEN ANCIENT, PROBLEM: THEN AND NOW

New knowledge of the natural world and/or a new level of control over our environment (technology) has always raised at least four kinds of ethical issues, all of which are found in some of the earliest written records of Western civilization, including the Hebrew Bible. I will briefly note the first three of these and spend somewhat longer discussing the fourth.

The first set of ethical issues raised by scientific discovery concerns deciding (1) what are the ethical uses of this new knowledge, and (2) who should make the decisions regarding what constitutes such ethical uses and how are they to be held accountable? Should such decisions be left to some combination of the market, the church, and the government, or to some set of formal procedural deliberations?

The second set of ethical issues relates to deciding how to justly allocate the inevitable gains and losses, both psychic and material, brought about by scientific progress. These include changes in income, status, wealth, and way of life, as well as access to new knowledge and those valued products and services produced as a result of it. This distributional problem has proven to be one of the most difficult ethical issues for societies to deal with, especially nowadays when economic activity is thought to be a quasi-autonomous and self-regulating sphere.

The third set of ethical issues involves deciding how to manage the undesirable side effects that always accompany new technologies. It is useful to keep in mind that one common reaction to humanity's ever-increasing powers and their associated responsibilities is pessimism. As Václav Havel is said to have noted, "ahead lies the abyss." Pessimism often reflects a revolt not only against the role of reason and scientific progress, but also against liberal democratic politics and their underlying cultural commitments. It is often associated with a willingness to believe the worst, and a belief that nature, undefiled by man, is sacred. The general anxiety that always surrounds change is likely to be elevated as we head into the so-called biological era, as there is no more personally intimate type of scientific development than those in biomedical science.

Surprising as it may be to some, many fear the consequences of the utopian search for ever better health. It releases fantasies of self-mastery and Promethean powers, and nightmares of evil eugenic strategies. Some feel that it is sinful to try to improve radically on God's masterwork, or that genetic research will lead to a genetic engineering industry dominated by values such as materialism, individual self-fulfillment, and profit as opposed to a social order based on justice, equality, and social solidarity. Ever since the Enlightenment, technology's critics have worried that our new powers are drawing us inexorably toward an autocratic state. More recently, this notion has been augmented by the suggestion that the combination of events on the biomedical frontier with a radical commitment to both individual choice and the moral ideal of self-fulfillment will lead to dystopia and a nightmare for humankind. Still others carry a general fear of and alienation from the modern world and its consequences. For this group, the future holds not the promise of more fully realizing our humanity, but the reverse. My own fear in this respect is that such pessimistic attitudes will lead to passivity and inaction.

Now I would like to deal with, at somewhat greater length, the fourth set of ethical issues provoked by major scientific discoveries. This is the inevitable need to decide whether new scientific knowledge "fits" or is consistent with the current human narrative. By the term *human narrative* I mean the revealed and/ or constructed story inevitably developed by every society to bestow some transcendental meaning on our individual and collective efforts. These narratives, grand and modest, rational or irrational, develop as a response to our own mortality, to our lack of control over aspects of our situation, and to the apparent insignificance of any individual. They represent both an effort to assure us that we are part of something meaningful beyond ourselves and a victory of hope over dread. They connect us to past and future generations, providing the continuity necessary for human flourishing. The human imagination seems to need to invest our history, our times, and our lives with meaning. It may be a thorny matter to invest history with meaning, but it is essential if we are to invest our efforts with beliefs and desires that go beyond ourselves. These narratives make it possible for us to deal with the insecurities of life and the certainty of death. I think of them as helping us shape our imaginations, form our aspirations, and construct a more rewarding reality. They also provide us with some moral guidance regarding which "authorities" to obey.

Either in place of, or as a supplement to, such narratives, human societies have long experimented with substances of various kinds that "transport" the individual away from the human condition as he or she is currently experiencing it to an "other-worldly" experience of some kind. This strategy brings only temporary relief and often undermines the work of more productive narratives. Finally, I should acknowledge that despite the depth, strength, and importance of these human narratives, critics of the status quo often criticize them as being mere quasi-coercive devices that enable the powerful to exploit the weak.

Narratives sustain our individual and joint efforts, contextualize our ethical norms, and are a more universal human characteristic than human curiosity. To me, they are essential for the survival of human communities. William James expressed this longing for a narrative when he talked of the human species' "indomitable desire to cast the world in a more rational state" or to give the sequence of events we experience a deeper meaning and sense of connection. Of course there have always been observers who thought that these narratives were mere fantasies. In *The Sanity of Art*, George Bernard Shaw (1908, pp. 58–59) expressed this viewpoint as follows: "We are afraid to look life straight in the face and see it, not the fulfillment of a moral law or of the deduction of reason, but the satisfaction of a passion in us of which we can give no rational account whatever." My perspective is that only such narratives can explain events that are either unique or cyclic on such a long time scale that they are quite beyond experiment. For all these reasons, narratives are not only ubiquitous but essential for human flourishing. Without such a narrative, or with a neurotic narrative, it would be difficult to elicit the kind of effort and sacrifice that communities require for their continued functioning. Such myths or other constructed and/or revealed narratives define our place in nature, give us a sense of purpose, and provide us with some moral guidance. They make a meaningful life possible by helping us understand how we should act, why we should act in that way, and whose interests are being served by particular actions. Although science has rather little to say either about the morality of our individual actions or the social customs and traditions that shape the world in which we live, it can speak directly to the nature of the parameters that need to govern important aspects of our human narratives.

These narratives, such as the ubiquitous creation narratives, are not only great feats of the human imagination, but have helped human societies transform the mundane into the wonderful. They help us give an account of ourselves, or of what it means to be human, that reaches beyond the notion that everything we care about and value consists only of mindless, meaningless physical particles or tiny vibrating strings. In a certain way they are like the genes that keep part of us alive even after our individual stories have ended. Like germ cells, narratives can live on to connect us and our efforts to both past and future generations. Indeed, these narratives represent our socially transmitted inheritance of behaviors, beliefs, and attitudes. They combine with our genetic and nongenetic inheritance and certain random elements to produce the diverse sets of human natures we observe in different communities.

In classical Greek and Roman society, it took the full pantheon of gods and their seemingly bizarre behaviors to give order and meaning to an often frightening and equally bizarre world. To be fair, it has always appeared to me that Newton's notions of gravity and Descartes's notion of consciousness were also invoked to explain the inexplicable. At other times, for other people, the great religions fulfilled this function. Religion is, as John F. Wilson (1982, p. 22) has noted, "A means by which a person fulfills existential needs." More generally, the world's great religions have been a powerful source of meaning for many, especially when things go wrong. The great narratives of the Bible, for example, deal with the issue of human origins and destiny through the basic themes of creation, salvation, and redemption. For a few millennia, these narratives have given meaning to the efforts and lives of many. Of course, the Bible provides a radically different framework regarding humankind's origin and ultimate destiny than certain more secular narratives. Although secular narratives often are more accommodating to a variety of beliefs, for many they contain insufficient content, provide too little moral guidance, and contain no internal assurance that matters will "work out." In any case, all narratives attempt to answer the questions posed by, among others, the painter Paul Gauguin (1897): *D'où venons-nous?* (Where do we come from?), *Qui sommes-nous?* (Who are we?), and *Où allons-nous?* (Where are we going?). They suggest, moreover, that we have a common fear of being cut off from memory, or set loose from the human stories that give meaning to life's experiences. To lose such moorings inevitably brings anxiety, loss, and confusion.

The challenge we now face is deciding how to adapt our current narratives regarding the meaning of human existence in light of our new understanding and scientific knowledge of both the natural world and our evolving concept(s) of "human nature." This is an especially important challenge when significant parameters of the human condition change, particularly if our new knowledge undermines the truth claims of existing narratives. The erosion of existing narratives threatens established identities, traditional life patterns, and, in some cases, the foundation of important social institutions and customs. The practical concern immediately arises: Where will we find the basis for a new narrative and a new morality to support it? To change a narrative requires great imagination and cultural innovation. Recall the warning of Friedrich Nietzsche, who noted, rather famously, that if God is dead, then anything can happen! Many then feared that the loss of theistic belief would result in moral collapse, and indeed some point to the sobering cost inflicted on humanity by twentieth-century authoritarian "utopias," such as Hitler's Germany and Stalin's Soviet Union. Others, however, look at the positive models that have developed and eagerly grasp the additional human responsibilities that have come with our new technological powers.

It is stunning to realize that many of these issues are present in Sophocles' play, *Antigone*, in, for example, the poem known as "Ode to Man." The poem is in the voice of a shepherd on a hillside who is watching a farmer deploy a new technology—namely, agriculture. On the one hand, the shepherd expresses admiration for human intelligence by noting that humankind is "clever beyond hope." On the other hand, he mourns the passing of a way of life occasioned by the then radically new agricultural technology, remarking, with some resignation, "May he [the farmer who slashes away at the goddess Mother Earth with his plow] never share my hearth." Tolstoy (1977, p. 134) expresses quite similar thoughts in his short story "Hadji Murat": "What a cruel destructive creature man is. How many living creatures and plants he has destroyed in order to support his own life, I thought, instinctively, looking for some sign of life in the midst of this dead black field." Similar sentiments have reappeared again and again in Western literature throughout the ages.

Early in *Antigone* Sophocles reflects on the difficulty of adjusting our narratives; in this same play he also addresses the issue of human "overstepping" or of engaging in "unnatural" activity, as Zeus constantly restrains the other gods from becoming too much like him. This same note is echoed both in the Prometheus legend, in which the god of fire and technology comes in for punishment for behaving in too godlike a fashion, and in the biblical narrative of the Tower of Babel. Recall also the ancient Greek legend regarding Argo, the first boat. The narrator of this legend not only worries about the loss of the pine trees required to build a boat, but, more important, about the release of unnatural desires, such as the desire to travel to new places. Indeed, the concept of "natural" human limits is built into many of the world's religions. Recall that the Old Testament taught that the desire for knowledge was responsible for the Fall of Man. In more recent works of fiction these ancient themes reappear. Various versions of the ever-popular Faust legend are focused either on a scientist who is doomed by his attempt, however noble, to overstep our God-given limitations, or a scientist who discovers that many things that give our life meaning are beyond the reach of science. In this latter respect, recall the words that Goethe (1992–98, vol. 2, p. 12) puts in the mouth of his Faust:

I've studied, alas, . . .
And how I regret it. . . .
With what result? Poor fool that I am,
I'm no whit wiser than when I began!

At the same time, we should recall that the public's view of scientists is ambivalent and subject to dramatic changes. In the English-speaking world, the impact of the accomplishments of Isaac Newton on the seventeenth-century psyche created the popular image of the scientist as a respected person of genius, or at least of great intellectual achievement. By the eighteenth century, however, the arrogant and godless scientist becomes a figure of satire, as in Alexander Pope's *Dunciad*, which attacks scientists for trying to replace God's law with their own. Pope felt that although scientists had the same moral failings as everyone else, their power made them more dangerous, even sinister. The Romantics, on the other hand, worried less about the potential misuse of science and focused on what they saw as scientists' limited agenda, which seemed to deny the validity of the emotions, spiritual longings, and individuality. In the nineteenth century, the notion of the scientist as a hero battling disease and powering a new prosperity took hold of the public imagination. Indeed, a new nexus developed involving science, capitalism, liberalism, change, and a feeling of cultural superiority among scientifically advanced nations. Even at that time, however, there were those, such as Jules Verne, who feared that scientists could become too egotistical, power-hungry, and socially irresponsible. In fact, at the early dawn of the scientific age, in the seventeenth and early eighteenth centuries, science and scientists were often the target of satire, as in Jonathan Swift's *Gulliver's Travels*. More recently (1911), George Bernard Shaw ridiculed (mistakenly) those scientists pursuing the implications of the germ theory of disease in his *Doctor's Dilemma*. On the other hand, books such as Sinclair Lewis's *Arrowsmith*, published in 1925, and certain twentieth-century films, such as *The Microbe Hunters* (1926), *The Story of Louis Pasteur* (1936), *Yellow Jack*

(1938), and *Doctor Ehrlich's Magic Bullet* (1940), have hailed scientists as heroic figures.

Most of our cultural traditions and the narratives that support them have two significant characteristics. First, they represent the human condition as set between two realms. There is the realm of those matters that are, at least in a moral sense, below us (i.e., the natural world, which, if we are well motivated, we can use and exploit, while it remains somehow "less" than we are in a moral sense). And there is that something "above us" that remains beyond human understanding. Perhaps Alexander Pope (1950, p. 13) was speaking, in part, of humankind's self-defined "middle" position when he wrote in *Essay on Man*: "Created half to rise, half to fall, Great Lord of all things, yet prey to all." The second general characteristic of these narratives is that they posit something unique about both the planet Earth, as compared to other celestial bodies, and human beings as compared to other forms of life. Any scientific development that undermines either of these two critical themes—the uniqueness of Earth and its inhabitants or our position "sandwiched" between forces beyond our understanding and a world subject to our exploitation—especially threatens our belief systems. The inevitable question thus arises: Are narratives typified by such themes still viable, in the sense of being able to inspire human effort?

Consider, for example, the psychic shocks occasioned by the work of Copernicus, Darwin, Freud, and contemporary genetics and cosmology. After Copernicus, the Earth could no longer be considered the center of the universe. After Darwin, the uniqueness of human beings seemed threatened. Recent developments in genetics seem to reaffirm this trend by showing that we share the same genetic code as all other living organisms. Freud discovered that, however unique we are, we are not even in charge of our own minds. Even the psychotropic drugs that have helped so many persons make it increasingly unclear just what *our real mind* refers to.

Finally, contemporary developments in astrophysics assure us that we are like a speck of dust in the universe slowly going

140

nowhere, though obeying the laws of thermodynamics. Others reject the notion that we are just milling about in a universe that has little meaning and is heading nowhere. They insist that human beings are more than the accidental result of genetic mutations and natural selection, and more, in a moral sense, than other living and nonliving things. In my view, our new understanding of the origin and the nature of the universe has great implications for our human narrative. For example, it seems to me that we can no longer easily speak of the meaningfulness of life, but only of how we may individually and collectively lead a meaningful life.

Although science may be able to do quite well without the assistance of a narrative that gives some transcendental meaning to human toil and effort, science alone cannot explain everything. In particular, it cannot tell us what is morally permissible or not permissible. It is left to the revealed and/or constructed narratives to tell us about what constraints on human freedom are necessary so that we may live together, lead meaningful lives, and take the interests of others into account when we act. The mounting ethical complexities faced by individuals in an era of rapid change are mirrored by the complexity of setting public policy in a morally pluralistic liberal democracy. Let me now turn, therefore, from the very ancient problem to the relatively new one.

THE RELATIVELY NEW PROBLEM

The relatively new challenge we face is how to resolve ethically contested issues in a society committed to cultural pluralism. A liberal democracy is many different things, but most agree that it is a system committed to, among other values, the rule of law, democratic self-government, private property, important limitations on government actions, equal protection, and freedom of speech, assembly, and religion. Moreover, a liberal democracy recognizes a variety of sources of authority in our lives, including not only the state, but also family and a variety of belief systems and cultural commitments A liberal state is, therefore, one with overlapping authority claims that must somehow be resolved. Even these characteristics, however, are not defined in some self-evident way. Considerable latitude exists among the liberal democracies, and even within a particular liberal democracy as to the exact social, cultural, and political arrangements.

Another important characteristic of liberal democracies that is often the source of considerable controversy is the notion of personal autonomy as an almost supreme value, the source of individual self-realization, and both a reflection of an authentic inner self and the source of our liberty. Moreover, in a regime of private markets, these notions of autonomy are further amplified or expressed by the economic freedoms to contract, use, and develop private property. This set of ideas is often set against the duties of culture, history, and tradition. Within this vision, morality is seen as grounded in individual moral agents who, as the autonomous bearers of rights, construct social arrangements that favor free choice over traditional moral commitments. In one way or another, according to this model, the mutual consent of individuals becomes the ultimate source of authority, rather than God, religion, history, traditionally rooted values, nature, or specially designated virtues. Along with this vision comes a fundamental commitment to the idea of moral pluralism—or, to put it somewhat differently, a rejection of moral tyranny. Indeed, a liberal democracy requires the state to show equal concern for all citizens, even those with divergent moral concepts.

I understand liberal democracy as a movement that gathered force with the Enlightenment, when moral and political philosophers despaired of producing a shared agreement regarding the goods to be pursued in the virtuous life. Gradually, society decided to leave this matter to individual choice, to make all individuals the authors of their own destiny. Indeed, the notion arose that the individual would come to be defined by the actual choices he or she made, and not according to the claims of tradition, culture, and history. Because individuals in such an environ-

142

ment are considered autonomous moral agents, they must be free to choose for themselves, as long as they do not harm the personal autonomy of others. Indeed, the very idea of personal autonomy is that persons must be free to choose for themselves in order to be able to act in an ethical fashion. The resulting collective conscience of liberal democracies is especially complex because it contains plural normative discourses and is characterized not only by a multiplicity of beliefs and sentiments, but also by the associated notion that all ideas and arrangements must constantly be reexamined and eventually be replaced by better ideas and social arrangements. Few welcome the idea that everything about our existence is temporary, yet that very idea is the source of great creativity in science and other areas of scholarship.

The historically rather startling implication of this situation is that in a liberal society, no particular set of beliefs occupies the moral high ground; rather, a number of coherent, thoughtful, and even compelling approaches to moral philosophy exist side by side, are inconsistent with each other, and compete for our allegiance. The moral and political challenge in such an environment is to define a social/political framework that allows citizens with different views to feel bound together by some type of common discourse while leaving undefined the ultimate moral basis for respecting another person's rights and views.

The essence of the moral pluralism that characterizes liberal democracies is the attitude that there is more than one thoughtful approach to the rules that we construct so that we may live together. Moral pluralism holds, in other words, that a number of important systems of ethical values and principles are each rationally defensible but mutually incompatible. In such a society, well-formed moral philosophies do not score "knockout" blows against each other, as do scientific theories, in a realm where well-defined rules determine the best of current theories. In moral philosophy, logically coherent if incomplete theories exist side by side, competing for our commitment and allegiance. As long as we enjoy free association and a capacity to think and act for ourselves, value conflicts will not be the result of selfishness, prejudice, ignorance, or poor reasoning, but rather will be the inevitable by-product of an environment in which well-intentioned citizens often disagree about complex moral and political issues. Compromise and accommodation must be the norm, because we recognize and value the integrity of others who do not share our beliefs.

In such a context there can be no easy public policy responses to complex or controversial ethical issues. The challenge of constructing morally coherent communities within liberal democracies is not a brand new problem, but, given the difficulty of accommodating different moral perspectives, the few short centuries we have had have not been enough practice. It is, therefore, a continuing experiment. Indeed, thoughtful observers today believe that this individualistic view of the human being is an outright fiction developed to promote particular social or political agendas. Some claim that the "reforms" spawned by the Enlightenment simply replaced one method of social control with another. Communitarians, for example, argue that the individual is embedded in a social reality that in large part defines the nature of his or her personhood. Other thoughtful observers believe that as a result of our commitment to moral pluralism we have lost what is essentially, good in any society—namely a sufficiently robust shared hierarchy of values. To take an obvious example, in America today we have widespread and bitter disagreement about the place of religion and religiously informed moral judgments in public life. More generally, we have deep differences regarding the source of our moral constraints and the optimal relationship of moral judgment to public policy. Communitarians believe that we must try much harder to define some process to articulate a shared structure, a ranking of goods and values sufficient to resolve moral debates on important matters. They often point out that individual rights are too sparse a concept to settle moral disputes on important matters. In any case, a liberal democracy with a serious commitment to moral pluralism must remain dedicated to a continuous process of social negotiation, not only regarding the moral basis for any restraint on individual freedom or the exact standing of the interests of others, but also regarding when such negotiations and decisions may be left to legislatures.

Other characteristics of liberal democracies generate additional levels of moral anxiety. The political and social attitude that underlies a liberal society supports free thinking, assumes open futures, and is always looking for better arrangements in our economic, social, and political life. This attitude is hostile to the status quo. Indeed, for liberals, doubt and change are quite noble things. Anticipation, suspense, and uncertainty suffuse the culture and become part of the "cost" of this new order. It is not happenstance, therefore, that the nineteenth century, which saw the first full flowering of liberal democracies, gave birth to the idea of a permanent revolution, whether of the Marxian or the liberal variety.

Meanwhile, those making public policy must also recognize that, however broad-based a society's commitment to liberal values may be, many people continue to look to authority and tradition for comfort or to minimize their moral losses in what they perceive to be an unstable and perhaps threatening environment. For one reason or another, many people are unable to visualize a time when the current set of social arrangements might need to be replaced. Although to a liberal, change means freedom, to many others, change continues to be a source of anxiety, even fear. In addition, liberal theory defines a very limited role for government in deciding the correct ethical and moral behavior for individuals. The principal roles of government in this respect are limited to protecting the personal autonomy of all citizens, deciding which risks should not be left to private bargains, correcting the undesirable impacts of an economic system left primarily to the forces of private property and private markets, and providing certain public goods. Accordingly, there are broad areas where it is not legitimate for the government to act, especially on matters of strong ethical disagreement. This limitation of government action is an especially strong norm in the United States, and is now supported by a substantial body of U.S. constitutional law. The result, in an era when scientific progress alone is providing a growing portfolio of ethical challenges, is considerable ongoing anxiety while liberal commitments to individual autonomy, moral pluralism, and a limited role for government continue to undermine existing arrangements of all kinds. Liberals such as I, who should be happy in the midst of the pain and loss that change always brings, need to understand how fearsome the liberal dream of individual autonomy and independence remains for many. In opting for liberal arrangements, we also are opting for a complex and anxious ethical environment.

Finally, we must recognize that contemporary Western culture is characterized by a bewildering kaleidoscope of identities, ethnicities, values, and cosmologies that are certain to generate a persistent array of tensions. In such a context, there are many incentives to avoid the high transaction costs of moral argument and social negotiation, and instead resort to a form of moralizing characterized by an inappropriate lack of humility (i.e., being too self-certain) and a tendency to try to force others to behave in certain ways. Even more dangerous is the tendency of moralizers to "purify society," no matter the cost.

Before I move on to discuss the "really new" problem we are facing, let me reiterate that the social arrangements of a liberal society are, I believe, central to the continuing vitality of both the research university and the world of science and scholarship. Of particular importance here is the liberal attitude that all ideas and arrangements will be replaced sooner or later by better options. In a liberal environment, there are no unquestionable or unquestioned ways of thinking. The enemy of scholarly inquiry (to say nothing about academic freedom and independence) is authority, especially absolute authority. It is no accident that liberal societies have been characterized by the enhanced vitality of the scholarly enterprise.

To summarize so far: During the age in which we live, science produces change, change produces anxiety and loss, and lots of scientific change produces lots of anxieties. In a time of rapid scientific change, we are bound to have to make difficult moral calculations, and to continue to search for effective ways to sustain our commitment to moral pluralism, free association, and the autonomy and worth of each individual. Let me turn now to the "really new" problem facing us in this regard.

THE "NEWEST" PROBLEM

The "newest" problem I have in mind quite simply is the radical nature of recent developments in human genetics. At the very least, these discoveries require us to revisit certain issues in moral philosophy that deal with what it means to be human and how we relate to the natural world, to one another, and to future generations. Indeed, earlier observers such as Aldous Huxley worried that the conquest of disease, aggression, pain, anxiety, suffering, and grief might bring in its wake a loss of the essence of our current understanding of the various human natures that now give meaning to our human experiences. Many today feel that new discoveries in human genetics require some significant change or adjustment in our current human narratives. This is especially true because it is not clear whether we are motivated to use these prospective new powers in order to liberate ourselves, normalize ourselves, improve ourselves, or change our social status.

Despite the complex interaction between genetic and environmental factors, the rising prospect of genetic medicine (the manipulation of the human genome to alter the distribution of phenotypical traits) raises for some the fearsome specter of eugenics. Many fear that our new reproductive choices will usher in a new eugenics subject to dangerous abuse not only in the form of state control of reproductive choices, but also in the form of our own enhanced ability to choose the kind of children we want, of our becoming "designing" parents. To some, the prospect of genetic engineering provides a new opportunity for transcendence. For

147

others, it threatens to undermine the very concept of what it means or should mean to be human.

Although few today are interested in resurrecting the "old" eugenics supported by a dangerous combination of social prejudice and naive science, some feel strongly that it will be very difficult to separate "good" medical genetics from the "bad" eugenics of the past. In any case, the prospect that society will somehow use this new knowledge to foster the breeding of so-called favorable traits and take steps, by law or by social norms, to prevent the breeding of those with so-called negative traits raises well-founded anxieties. For many, this development threatens to repeat the folly of trying to deal with social problems by exclusively technical means.

In these respects, we can recall that Somerset Maugham's novel, *The Magician* (1908) portrays a scientist obsessed with a desire to vie with God by creating embryos, even if it requires him to sacrifice his new wife. And Karel Capek's play *R.U.R.* (1933) also portrays a scientist trying to "play God" by creating humans in a radically nontraditional manner. Recall also that a great majority of horror films feature the theme of new science falling into evil hands. In these more recent works of film and fiction, an ancient theme reappears, namely, that it is ethically dangerous to overstep "natural" human limits.

Contemporary developments in genetics also bring us closer and closer to the "Genesis problem": the potential, as already noted, to exert much greater control over how many people exist, when people come into existence, what their identities as persons will be, and the length and quality of their lives. Such powers raise a number of questions. For example, do such interventions benefit or harm the people we bring into existence? Are we morally obligated to prevent the existence of those who will be seriously disabled? In any case, what set of characteristics, exactly, creates a "disability"? Would the genetic enhancement of a person's cognitive, physical, and emotional capacities above the normal level of functioning (motivated by perfectionism rather than by justice or beneficence) be morally objectionable? This latter question raises the broader ethical question of any act motivated by perfectionism. Should we, for example, consider the use of psychotropic medications to be an inappropriate violation of or appropriate restoration of our true identities? What state represents our authentic selves? Why do we feel uneasy about athletes who use steroids but not about children who receive vaccinations? These and other ethical questions inevitably remind us that our new powers bring with them new issues, new responsibilities, and the need for an appropriate set of values to govern our decisions using them.

Also, we need to think carefully about the impact of any eventual capacity to alter genes passed on to the next generation and of newly discovered genetic bases of behaviors on our notion of individual autonomy. Individual autonomy and self-realization are two of the key foundations of our liberal democracy. Any limitations on the individual's capacity for self-realization, genetically based or otherwise, are matters of concern. (Admittedly, limitations can arise from a large variety of nongenetic sources, including inadequate psychological resources, inadequate financial endowments, inadequate care, and discrimination.)

Although such questions bring us close to the issue of what it means to be human, we should continue to recall that there is no single immutable human nature, but a large variety of human natures, bequeathed to us over time by the many different cultures and environments that have populated our planet. Nevertheless, these and similar questions are arising now with a new urgency because knowledge of the probable effects of a given action (e.g., to prescreen and selectively abort or fail to implant certain embryos) or lack of action (e.g., not to screen, or not to selectively abort) have already given us a certain measure of control over those effects, and control over effects is a necessary condition for being responsible for them. Clearly, our actions today in both the scientific and cultural sphere will profoundly affect the evolutionary future of our own species.

PUBLIC BIOETHICS AND PUBLIC POLICY

Before dealing directly with the issue of bioethics and public policy, I would like to characterize some central elements of the environment in which public policy is formulated in the United States. The most obvious elements of this environment are its complexity, its uncertain direction, its opportunism, and the randomness with which the action agenda is shaped. The path of public policy is like that of a young river that has not yet selected its course—even though its general drift may seem clear. Those involved in the public policy process seldom see it this way, because they are too busy identifying problems (never in short supply), working out solutions (many incompatible with one another), and hoping for the political moment when action may be possible. The first difficulty, as John Kingdon (1995) has pointed out, is that the problem identifiers, the problem solvers, and the political actors operate in quite separate communities.

The arrival of the right political moment for action is the most unpredictable element of all. That, added to the strong American preference for not only a limited but also a fragmented system of government, makes it relatively difficult for the government to provide the public goods (e.g., environmental protection) required by advanced industrialized societies.

In this public policy environment I want to highlight something I call "public bioethics." By this term I mean the process of deriving public policy propositions regarding bioethics via the deliberations of officially appointed groups of experts and other thoughtful citizens, such as the National Bioethics Advisory Commission (NBAC) appointed by President Clinton, which I chaired. Why should we have such groups? Some of the reasons are as follows:

1. To add needed expertise to the process of public policy formation;

2. To deflect conflict away from the presidential administration and Congress;

3. To appear "presidential" by asking for the opinion of others;

4. To appear to be active on an issue without actually taking any action beyond appointing the committee;

5. Temporarily to forestall actions by either the administration or Congress;

6. To solicit an endorsement of one's views by judicious selection of "independent" outsiders.

Further, why should such groups meet in public? Many citizens are against, even aghast at, the idea of public deliberations as the basis of constructing public policies in ethically contentious arenas. My own experience is that, whenever it is possible, it is healthy to meet in public, especially in a deliberative democracy and especially with respect to morally contested issues. The public nature of the resulting discourse has a number of advantages:

1. It disciplines group discussion in the sense that it encourages thinking before talking;

2. It enables the group to receive more relevant input and feedback from all interested parties;

3. It provides an opportunity and a forum to demonstrate respect for other views on controversial issues;

4. And, finally, it may provide added legitimacy to any subsequent government actions.

In this overall context, let me reflect for a few moments on how a particular exercise in public bioethics evolved. The NBAC of 1996 to 2001 dealt with the issues of reproductive cloning (the "Dolly" issue) and of the research employing human embryonic stem cells. These issues brought to the fore the area of the deepest moral divide in American political life: the abortion debate. The issues that surround this debate include what some believe to be the sacred nature of the process of reproduction and the moral status of both the fertilized ovum and the early embryo. In the United States, the first public policy concern in these areas was not whether or not cloning, or research utilizing human embryonic cells, should be legal, but whether the U.S.

government itself should, from an ethical perspective, sponsor research that might involve the destruction of very early embryos, or provide "inappropriate intervention" in the process of human reproduction. I will deal, first, with the formation of possible public policy responses to the Dolly experiment.

The "Dolly" Issue

The most immediate reason for constructing some type of public policy response to the "Dolly" experiment was the initial public hysteria that greeted the news of Dolly's birth. Although some aspects of this hysteria may seem quaint now, it was very real at the time and involved uninformed statements issued by some quarters of the scientific community that revealed a lack of knowledge of significant findings that had accumulated for decades regarding the DNA content of cells.

Beyond the hysteria, misinformation, and rhetoric that seemed to provide support for discredited notions of genetic determinism, there was an additional and well-articulated set of concerns that the use of this technology for human reproduction would undermine our sense of individuality, our uniqueness, our "human nature."

In any case, immediately following the news of the Dolly experiment, the NBAC received a call from the White House, and we were asked to report our recommendations within ninety days. We proceeded as follows: First, we solicited advice and counsel from a wide variety of experts. Second, we looked for ways to triage the issue in order to select the aspects we could deal with in the time constraints set by the president.

With respect to advice, we first asked a number of scientists to brief the committee on the scientific issues involved. Next, we looked to moral philosophers to gain some inspiration and insight on how we might deal with the ethical issues involved, particularly those of moral status and the threat to personal identity and self-worth. We also turned to a wide variety of religious leaders and scholars to see if they could help us think through these same issues and inform us of their views on the matter. Finally, we solicited the views of the scientific community and others on the public policy issues involved.

A number of things became clear almost immediately. First, although moral philosophy and theology provided us with many tools and a great deal of inspiration with which to analyze the issues, the conclusions and advice of the various moral philosophers and theologians we consulted matched the full spectrum of public opinion. Indeed, advice on what constituted ethical use of this new technology varied from the requirement to use the technique as if it were safe and morally worthy, to the position that it was per se a sin to engage in such "unnatural" or "godlike" activity. Second, the scientific community's principal concern remained its traditional one—namely, for the public to provide the resources but not interfere with the scientific agenda. Finally, it was almost immediately apparent that, at the time, the procedure itself was demonstrably unsafe and its impact not fully understood.

The obvious safety issues (to both mother and developing fetus) made it quite easy to address the short-term public policy issues. It was also quite clear that moral philosophy alone could not provide a compelling enough case to solve the public policy problem. We could even put aside, for the moment, both the constitutional issue of whether the Supreme Court would allow any regulation in the reproductive arena by the states or federal government and careful evaluation of the growing literature on the experience of natural clones, namely, identical twins. Moreover, given our time constraints, previous studies, and political realities, we decided not to revisit the issues surrounding embryo-splitting, or embryo research, including issues surrounding the work of fertility clinics, all matters that raise ethical issues similar to the prospect of human cloning using the "Dolly technique."

Our decision, therefore, was to focus only on the use of somatic cell nuclear transfer cloning for the specific purpose of creating an infant. Here was a case where the long-run ethical issues were difficult to assess, but where the immediate ethical and public policy imperatives were quite easy to identify. Our conclusion was that at the current time, because of the many safety issues, it was ethically unacceptable to use this technology in the public or private sector to create a child. Although in our minds the safety issues were the paramount ethical issue of concern, we also believed it necessary to encourage further public discussion and to do further scientific research. For one thing, it was not entirely clear how it would be ethically possible to demonstrate the safety of this technique for reproducing a human. Having reached this decision, the only remaining controversial issue was whether legislation was advisable, because this is what would be required to cover both the public and private sectors, or whether an executive order that would cover only the expenditure of public funds and then hope to encourage voluntary restraint in the private sector was the best public policy choice. We opted for the former strategy, which, events have demonstrated, was a tactical error.

Human Embryonic Stem Cells

The ability to isolate and culture human embryonic stem cells was an important scientific achievement that immediately generated both excitement and concern. As with the "Dolly" issue, many had forgotten that scientists had known for some time that we contain self-renewing and multipotent cells and that in mammals embryonic stem cells had a great deal of multipotency. Let me now turn to the ethical issues surrounding research that involves the creation and use of human embryonic stem cells. Such research involves the destruction of embryos in order to isolate the stem cells. What moral obligations, if any, do we have with respect to the fertilized ovum and the so-called early embryo? Specifically, this debate raises central issues such as:

1. Does even the very early embryo enjoy the moral status of a live born child?

2. If so, is its purposeful destruction for any reason an act of homicide?

3. If not, what state protections should it benefit from, if any?

4. Is it logically possible to say when "human life" begins and if "human life" needs protection only at certain stages of development?

Opponents of embryonic stem cell research generally support the view that the embryo, at all stages of its development, has the moral status of a live born child. Moreover, they often remind us of the sacredness of human life, which, in their view, begins with the fertilized ovum. Given such beliefs, they cannot sanction the destruction of the embryo merely for the sake of scientific or clinical progress, because it involves the "murder" of innocents. Many others including myself believe, on the other hand, that our moral obligations to the fertilized ovum and early embryo are not that comprehensive. I have often thought that for persons of faith it must be a little disconcerting, even idolatrous, to assign to any object, including human life, "sacred" or godlike status. Moreover, in a society that freely practices war and capital punishment, encourages in vitro fertilization clinics, and tolerates inadequate nourishment of young children, the emphasis on the "sacredness" of the life of early embryos seems to me to have a rather empty ring to it. Furthermore, such concerns, whether valid or not, must be dealt with in the context of another ethical imperative—namely, to do what we can to relieve the burden of disease from present and future generations.

For some, it is very hard to find the right balance between a commitment to protect human life at all stages of development with a generally shared ethical commitment to further the development of better clinical modalities in medicine. Such a tension would, of course, vanish if other research strategies, involving adult or placental stem cells, were equally useful or if one's moral commitment to the early-stage embryo trumped all other considerations. Given current scientific understanding and existing technological capacities, there are no easy solutions to this challenge. Therefore, research on human embryonic stem cells not only continues to raise serious and complex ethical issues, but does so in an area that has long polarized Americans.

How do these serious ethical questions involve public policy? First, the government, as a significant sponsor of biomedical research, may have to satisfy even higher ethical hurdles than private individuals and organizations because its actions implicate all citizens. Second, the state has a significant interest in whether or not public funds are involved, because the protection of life—and the possible prevention of homicide—may be involved. Finally, the government has an important mediating role when the public is sharply divided on important ethical issues. It is, therefore, important for public policy to reflect some type of stand on the ethical issues at stake.

To illustrate how actual public policy evolved over time, it is instructive to compare the NBAC's recommendations in this arena with the policies of the Clinton administration. Our group encouraged the use of federal funds to support both the creation and use of human embryonic stem cells in biomedical research, with some restrictions regarding consent and the source of these embryos. The Clinton administration, on the other hand, advocated a kind of "don't ask, don't tell" policy, with the use of federal funds being restricted to the use of human embryonic cell lines created by others. The Clinton administration's policy seemed to say that those who demand and pay for the destruction of embryos can be ethically isolated from those who actually do the deed! In principle, the policy permitted research with embryonic stem cell lines to be sponsored by the federal government. However, because these stem cell lines were controlled by private interests, the participation of university-based scientists depended on the nature of licensing agreements the private firms might insist on and the openness required by university policies. The subsequent evolution of this policy can now be seen in the Bush administration, which has mandated that federal sponsorship of embryonic stem cell research be restricted to those cell lines derived prior to August 9, 2001. Clearly, this process and policy is still very fluid. Although I prefer the position of the Clinton administration to that of the Bush administration, the Bush administration's policy is more ethically coherent. Both, however, limit the possibilities for participation by a significant proportion of the nation's leading biomedical scientists. This is a serious cost in view of the very considerable scientific challenges that still need to be overcome before we can realize the potential of embryonic stem cells to provide new clinical modalities.

The issue of human embryonic stem cell research has also been very controversial in the United Kingdom, involving many debates in both houses of Parliament. There, however, the government has developed a much more coherent, thoughtful, and publicly transparent policy, regulating stem cell and associated research areas in a uniform manner in both the public and private sectors. In the United States, on the other hand, it is "anything goes" in the private sector and severe restrictions in the public sector. One result of this policy is that here in America we have very little idea of what is going on. Second, although it is quite legal both to create and to use new embryonic stem cell lines for biomedical research in the United Kingdom, all such activities require a license, available only if the proposed research passes scientific muster, if appropriate consent is obtained, and if alternative approaches are less promising. In Britain, therefore, the entire enterprise is open to full public scrutiny.

The German Embryo Protection Act, unlike either the American or the British policy, prohibits all in vitro experimentation on the human embryo that is not in the interests of the embryo itself, thus prohibiting the production of human embryonic cell lines. The Universal Declaration on Human Rights and the Human Genome, adopted by the United Nations Educational, Scientific and Cultural Oranization on November 11, 1997, does not take a position on the moral status of the embryo. In all nations, public or international policy is trying to balance two competing ethical claims—our ethical obligation to relieve human suffering and disease and our ethical obligation to give the utmost respect to all forms of human "life."

CONCLUSION

One of our great responsibilities in the twenty-first century is to consider the social and human repercussions of our rapidly accumulating new knowledge and the appropriate response of public policy. Whatever one's views on the ultimate impact of advances in biomedical science on the evolving human condition, all thoughtful citizens need to consider their ongoing impact on the institutions, values, and other cultural commitments that sustain our individual and common life. The quality of our society will be determined by the moral norms that science and technology genuinely aspire to reflect.

Science is a social institution, and the application of science is a social decision. The world of science and the world of meaning are inextricably linked. Indeed, the scientist, the poet, and the philosopher share closely related goals. The scientist's search for ultimate causes, and the creative artist's search for the ultimate realities of our experience are similar quests, at least emotionally. Both try to draw together in a comprehensible fashion aspects of the natural world and human experience. At their best, both require deep reflection, a broad imagination, a certain humility, and a willingness to experiment with disconcerting ideas. Thoughtful accounts of the human condition share many characteristics, whether they are generated in the laboratory, the library, the scholar's study, or the narratives that give meaning to all that we do.

However, we face a significant quandary. Even thoughtful observers agree little on the relative importance of the various ethical and theological issues raised by new scientific developments, which philosophical approach is most relevant, or how any particular approach might inform public policy or private action. Indeed, there seems to be little convergence on either the right questions or the right answers. Thus, we are often unable to arrive at a consensus solely through a process of philosophical reasoning and deliberation. We have to reach actual decisions in some other way or we have to accept the fact that we may not always fully resolve some of the more contested nuances and difficult issues. Anxiety and ethical controversy, therefore, will continue to accompany us on this journey. It is particularly important to find venues for serious conversations between scientists and nonscientists, where all participants leave open the possibility of changing their minds. Moreover, it may be time for scientists to take the initiative in these matters, because their knowledge gives them special responsibilities.

Over history, different professions have been considered to have special responsibilities and, to some extent, authority in the moral realm. Indeed, at times these special moral commitments took the form of formalized oaths, although most often they were the expression of certain moral traditions and responsibilities accepted as one sign of professional responsibilities. Perhaps we are at a moment when scientists should feel a special responsibility to help society deal with the ethical issues being generated by the great successes taking place daily on the scientific frontier.

Perhaps the principal lessons of all this are the following:

1. The expressed anxieties we hear are real. Not only do scientists need to educate others about the potential and limitations of science, but scientists need to listen to the public's deep distress and consider the special limitations of science in dealing with issues of meaning.

2. We should not confuse what we can do or are doing with what we should do. We need to confront the ethical uses of deciding exactly how to use new knowledge.

3. In liberal democratic societies, the special public policy challenge is to know when it is legitimate and useful for the government to act and, when it is, which instruments—for example, regulations, legislation, and incentives—should be deployed.

4. Living an ethical life and setting public policies in ethically contested areas requires both individuals and policy makers constantly to carry out complex moral calculations.

159

5. The world of science and the world of meaning are so closely connected that realizing the potential of one requires dealing with the other.

This latter conclusion has important implications for the university's teaching programs. It provides yet another dimension to the argument that we need to lower the barriers between disciplines, between graduate and undergraduate education, and between professional education and the rest of the university. If we are going to have serious conversations between scientists and nonscientists, they will have to have a capacity to share a common language and understand each other's hopes and aspirations. Universities can contribute by designing curricula that allow for such disciplined and informed conversations throughout a student's experience on the campus.

Both those driving the biomedical frontier ahead and other thoughtful citizens share a common concern in finding a way to deploy this new knowledge in a manner that not only gives it moral content and human meaning, but relieves anxiety about the future. After all, what makes humans special, if not unique, is our highly developed potential for empathy, or, to put the matter more generally, the potential to put ourselves in the minds of others and to understand what they believe and desire. If scientists put themselves in the minds of nonscientists and vice versa, we may understand each other's needs and beliefs better. This is what ethics is all about. It remains central to our ability to adapt our narratives and belief systems to our increased understanding of the natural world.

If those advancing the scientific frontier wish to reach out to the public for support, understanding, and trust, they will have to understand and address the anxieties that are certain to continue to characterize public concerns and influence public policy. The values of science cannot be separated from the values of society. The vitality of the scientific enterprise can only be sustained if the society at large is committed to it. Most important, like artists, scientists and nonscientists engaged in thinking carefully about the future of the human condition cannot escape the anguish and uncertainty involved in trying to create a better future, especially when the ethical questions go to the heart of what it means to be human. Remember: it is difficult to understand who we humans really are, even harder to know what we should be, and most daunting of all to perceive who we might, or should, become.

❖ Bibliography ❖

Altbach, P. G., R. O. Berdahl, and P. J. Gumport, eds. 1994. *Higher Education in American Society*. Amherst, N.Y.: Prometheus Books.

The American Academic Profession. 1997. Special issue of *Daedalus* 126, no. 4 (Fall).

Bacon, F. 1861–74. "Preface to *The Great Instauration*." In *The Letters and the Life of Francis Bacon, Including All His Occasional Work*, ed. J. Spedding, vol. 4, pp. 117–21. London.

Balderston, F. E. 1995. *Managing Today's University: Strategies for Viability, Change, and Excellence*. 2nd ed. San Francisco: Jossey-Bass.

Baldwin, J. W. 1971. *The Scholastic Culture of the Middle Ages*. Lexington, Mass.: D. C. Heath.

Barrow, C. W. 1990. *Universities and the Capitalist State: Corporate Liberalism and the Reconstruction of American Higher Education, 1894–1928*. Madison: University of Wisconsin Press.

Barry, B. 2001. *Culture and Equality*. Cambridge, Mass.: Harvard University Press.

Barzun, J. 1993. *The American University: How It Runs, Where It Is Going*. Chicago: University of Chicago Press.

Baumol, W. J., S.A.B. Blackman, and E. N. Wolff. 1989. *Productivity and American Leadership*. Cambridge, Mass.: MIT Press.

Bender, T., and C. E. Schorske, eds. 1997. *American Academic Culture in Transformation: Fifty Years, Four Disciplines*. Foreword by S. R. Graubard. Princeton, N.J.: Princeton University Press.

Berube, M., and C. Nelson, eds. 1995. *Higher Education under Fire: Politics, Economics, and the Crisis of the Humanities*. New York: Routledge.

Bledstein, B. J. 1976. *The Culture of Professionalism: The Middle Class and the Development of Higher Education in America*. New York: Norton.

Bok, D. 1982. *Beyond the Ivory Tower: Social Responsibilities of the Modern University*. Cambridge, Mass.: Harvard University Press.

Bowen, W. G. 1987. *Ever the Teacher*. Princeton, N.J.: Princeton University Press.

Bowen, W. G., T. I. Nygren, S. E. Turner, and E. A. Duffy. 1994. *The Charitable Nonprofits: An Analysis of Institutional Dynamics and Characteristics*. San Francisco: Jossey-Bass.

Bowen, W. G., and H. T. Shapiro, eds. 1998. *Universities and Their Leadership*. Princeton, N.J.: Princeton University Press.

Bowen, W. G., and J. A. Sosa. 1989. *Prospects for Faculty in the Arts and Sciences: A Study of Factors Affecting Demand and Supply, 1987–2012*. Princeton, N.J.: Princeton University Press.

Boyle, R. 1670. "New Pneumatical Experiments about Respiration." *Philosophical Transactions* 5: 2044.

Brademas, J., with L. P. Brown. 1987. *The Politics of Education: Conflict and Consensus on Capital Hill*. Norman: University of Oklahoma Press.

Brodie, K., and L. Banner. 1996. *Keeping an Open Door: Passages in a University Presidency*. Durham, N.C.: Duke University Press.

Brown, P. 1969. *Augustine of Hippo*. Berkeley and Los Angeles: University of California Press.

Brubacher, J. S., and W. Rudy. 1976. *Higher Education in Transition: A History of American Colleges and Universities, 1636–1976*. 3rd ed. New York: Harper Collins.

Buchanan, A. 1985. *Ethics, Efficiency, and the Market*. Totowa, N.J.: Rowman & Allanheld.

Buchner, E. F. 1904. *The Educational Theory of Immanuel Kant*. Philadelphia: J. B. Lippincott.

Budig, G. A. 1992. *A Higher Education Map for the 1990s*. New York: Macmillan.

Capek, K. 1933. *R.U.R.* Garden City, N.Y.: Doubleday.

Carnegie Foundation for the Advancement of Teaching. 1990. *Campus Life: In Search of Community*. Foreword by E. L. Boyer. Princeton, N.J.: Carnegie Foundation for the Advancement of Teaching.

Chadwick, O. 1975. *The Secularization of the European Mind in the 19th Century*. Cambridge, U.K.: Cambridge University Press.

Chapman, G. 1998. "Will Technology Commercialize Higher Learning?" *Los Angeles Times*, Jan. 19.

Chapman, J. W. 1983. *The Western University on Trial*. Berkeley and Los Angeles: University of California Press.

Clark, B. R. 1983. *The Higher Education System: Academic Organization in Cross-National Perspective*. Berkeley and Los Angeles: University of California Press.

———, ed. 1987. *Perspectives on Higher Education: Eight Disciplinary and Comparative Views.* Berkeley and Los Angeles: University of California Press.

———. 1993. *The Research Foundations of Graduate Education: Germany, Britain, France, United States, Japan.* Berkeley and Los Angeles: University of California Press.

———. 1995. *Places of Inquiry: Research and Advanced Education in Modern Universities.* Berkeley and Los Angeles: University of California Press.

———. 1997. "The Modern Integration of Research Activities with Teaching and Learning." *Journal of Higher Education* 68, no. 3 (May–June): 241–55.

Clotfelter, C. T. 1992. *Who Benefits from the Nonprofit Sector?* Chicago: University of Chicago Press.

———. 1996. *Buying the Best: Cost Escalation in Elite Higher Education.* Princeton, N.J.: Princeton University Press.

Clotfelter, C. T., R. G. Ehrenberg, M. Getz, and J. J. Siegfried. 1991. *Economic Challenges in Higher Education.* Chicago: University of Chicago Press.

Cohen, A. M. 1998. *The Shaping of American Higher Education: Emergence and Growth of the Contemporary System.* San Francisco: Jossey-Bass.

Cohen, M. D., and J. G. March. 1986. *Leadership and Ambiguity: The American College President.* 2nd ed. Boston: Harvard Business School Press.

Collins, F. 1995. "The Human Genome Project." In *Life at Risk: The Crisis in Medical Ethics*, ed. R. D. Lamb and L. A. Moore, pp. 100–113. Nashville: Broadman and Holman.

Committee on the Objectives of a General Education in a Free Society. 1945. *General Education in a Free Society: A Report of the Harvard Committee.* Cambridge, Mass.: Harvard University Press.

Dickeson, R. C. 1999. *Prioritizing Academic Programs and Services: Reallocating Resources to Achieve Strategic Balance.* Foreword by S. O. Ikenberry. San Francisco: Jossey-Bass.

Die Zukunft der Geistes- und Sozialwissenschaften in Landern Mittelosteuropas unter Berucksichtigung von Erfahrungen aus dem deutschen Einigungsprozess—The Future of Humanities and Social Sciences in Central Eastern European Countries with Consideration of Experiences from the German Unification Process. 1995. DAAK-

GAAC Symposium Halle (Salle), 1–4 November 1995. Publications of the GAAC Symposia, vol. 3 (1995). Bonn–Washington, D.C.: DAAK-GAAC.

Distinctively American: The Residential Liberal Arts Colleges. 1999. Special issue of *Daedalus* 128, no. 1 (Winter).

Douglas, J. A. 2000. *The California Idea and American Higher Education, 1850 to the 1960 Master Plan.* Stanford, Calif.: Stanford University Press.

DuBois, W.E.B. 1903. *The Souls of Black Folks: Essays and Sketches.* Chicago: A. C. McClurg.

Duderstadt, J. J., D. E. Atkins, and D. Van Houweling. 2002. *Higher Education in the Digital Age: Technology Issues and Strategies for American Colleges and Universities.* Westport, Conn.: Praeger.

Duderstadt, J. J., H. T. Shapiro, F. Popoff, S. Olswang, and P. C. Hillegonds. 1995–96. *Changing in a World of Change: The University and Its Publics.* A series of addresses by the Senate Assembly and the Office of the President, University of Michigan.

Ehrenberg, R. G. 1997. *The American University: National Treasure or Endangered Species?* Ithaca, N.Y.: Cornell University Press.

Ehrlich, T., with J. Frey. 1995. *The Courage to Inquire: Ideals and Realities in Higher Education.* Bloomington: Indiana University Press.

Fallon, D. 1980. *The German University.* Boulder: Colorado Associated University Press.

Finkelstein, M. 1984. *The American Academic Profession: A Synthesis of Scientific Inquiry since World War II.* Columbus: Ohio State University Press.

Finkelstein, M. 1993. "From Tutor to Academic Scholar: Academic Professionalism in Eighteenth and Nineteenth Century America." *History of Higher Education Annual* 3: 99–121.

Flawn, P. T. 1990. *A Primer for University Presidents: Managing the Modern University.* Austin: University of Texas Press.

Fleming, R. W. 1996. *Tempests into Rainbows: Managing Turbulence.* Ann Arbor: University of Michigan Press.

Flexner, A. 1908. *The American College: A Criticism.* New York: Century.

Foner, E. 1990. *The New American History.* Philadelphia: Temple University Press.

Freedman, J. O. 1987. "A Commonwealth of Liberal Learning." Inaugural address delivered at Freedman's installation as the fifteenth president of Dartmouth College.

The Future of the Government/University Partnership. 1996. Proceedings of the 1996 Jerome B. Wiesner Symposium, ed. G. D. Krenz. Ann Arbor: University of Michigan.

Gauguin, P. 1897. *Where Do We Come From? What Are We? Where Are We Going?* Oil on canvas. Tompkins Collection, Boston Museum of Fine Arts.

Geiger, R. L. 1986. *To Advance Knowledge: The Growth of American Research Universities.* New York: Oxford University Press.

———. 1993. *Research and Relevant Knowledge: American Research Universities since World War II.* New York: Oxford University Press.

Giamatti, A. B. 1988. *A Free and Ordered Space: The Real World of the University.* New York: Norton.

Glassick, C. E., M. T. Huber, and G. I. Maeroff. 1997. *Scholarship Assessed: Evaluation of the Professoriate.* An Ernest L. Boyer Project of the Carnegie Foundation for the Advancement of Teaching. San Francisco: Jossey-Bass.

Gless, D. J., and B. H. Smith. 1992. *The Politics of Liberal Education.* Durham, N.C.: Duke University Press.

Goethe, J. W. von. 1992–98. *Faust.* Trans. M. Greenberg. 2 vols. New Haven, Conn.: Yale University Press.

Goodchild, L. F., and H. S. Wechsler, eds. 1997. *ASHE Reader on the History of Higher Education.* 2nd ed. Needham Heights, Mass.: Simon & Schuster Custom Publishing.

Grafton, A., and L. Jardine. 1986. *From Humanism to the Humanities: Education and the Liberal Arts in Fifteenth- and Sixteenth-Century Europe.* Cambridge, Mass.: Harvard University Press.

Graham, H. D., and N. Diamond. 1997. *The Rise of American Research Universities: Elites and Challengers in the Postwar Era.* Baltimore: Johns Hopkins University Press.

Grant, G., and D. Riesman. 1978. *The Perpetual Dream: Reform and Experiment in the American College.* Chicago: University of Chicago Press.

Hamlin, A. T. 1981. *The University Library in the United States.* Philadelphia: University of Pennsylvania Press.

Hanson, K. H., and J. W. Meyerson. 1990. *Higher Education in a Changing Economy.* New York: Macmillan.

Hanson, K. H., and J. W. Meyerson, eds. 1995. *International Challenges to American Colleges and Universities: Looking Ahead*. Phoenix: Oryx Press.

Haskins, C. H. 1990. *The Rise of Universities*. 18th ed. Ithaca, N.Y.: Cornell University Press.

Henry, J. B., and C. H. Scharff. 1996. *College As It Is, or The Collegian's Manual in 1853*. Ed. J. J. Looney. Princeton, N.J.: Princeton University Libraries.

Herbst, J. 1981. "Church, State and Higher Education: College Government in the American Colonies and States before 1820." *History of Higher Education Annual* 1: 42–54.

Hirsch, W. Z., and L. E. Weber. 1999. *Challenges Facing Higher Education at the Millennium*. Phoenix: Oryx Press.

Hofstadter, R. 1952. *The Development and Scope of Higher Education in the United States*. New York: Columbia University Press.

———. 1996. *Academic Freedom in the Age of the College*. Introduction by R. L. Geiger. New Brunswick, N.J.: Transaction.

Hofstadter, R., and W. Smith, eds. 1961. *American Higher Education: A Documentary History*. 2 vols. Chicago: University of Chicago Press.

Houellebecq, M. *The Elementary Particles*. Trans. F. Wynne. New York: Knopf, 2000.

Huxley, T. 1934. *Readings from Huxley*. Ed. C. Rinaker. New York: Harcourt, Brace.

In Praise of Libraries. 1989. New York: New York University Press.

Jencks, C., and D. Riesman. 1968. *The Academic Revolution*. New York: Doubleday.

Johnson, H. W. 1999. *Holding the Center: Memoirs of a Life in Higher Education*. Cambridge, Mass.: MIT Press.

Kaplin, W. A., and B. A. Lee. 1995. *The Law of Higher Education: A Comprehensive Guide to Legal Implications of Administrative Decision Making*. 3rd ed. San Francisco: Jossey-Bass.

Kennedy, D. 1998. *Academic Duty*. Cambridge, Mass.: Harvard University Press.

Kerr, C. 1963. *The Uses of the University*. The Godkin Lectures at Harvard University. Cambridge, Mass.: Harvard University Press.

———. 2001–3. *The Gold and the Blue: A Personal Memoir of the University of California, 1949–67*, vol. 1, *Academic Triumphs*; vol.

2, *Political Turmoil*. Berkeley and Los Angeles: University of California Press.

Kimball, B. A. 1995. *Orators and Philosophers: A History of the Idea of Liberal Education*. The College Board Forum on Standards and Learning. New York: College Entrance Examination Board.

———. *Voices from the Liberal Tradition: A Documentary History with Introductions, Notes, and Many New Translations*, vol. 1, *Origin to the End of the 1500s*; vol. 2, *1602 to the Twenty-first Century*. Unpublished manuscript.

Kingdon, J. 1995. *Agendas, Alternatives, and Public Policies*. Boston, Mass.: Addison-Wesley.

Kirkland, J. T. 1818. "Literary Institutions, University, Library." *North American Review* 8: 191–200.

Kors, A. C., and H. A. Silverglate. 1998. *The Shadow University: The Betrayal of Liberty on America's Campuses*. New York: Free Press.

Leslie, W. B. 1992. *Gentlemen and Scholars: College and Community in the "Age of the University," 1865–1917*. University Park: Pennsylvania State University Press.

Levine, A., ed. 1994. *Higher Learning in America, 1980–2000*. Baltimore: Johns Hopkins University Press.

Levine, D. O. 1987. *The American College and the Culture of Aspiration, 1915–1940*. Ithaca, N.Y.: Cornell University Press.

Lewis, S. 1998. *Arrowsmith*. New York: Penguin.

Light, R. J. 2001. *Making the Most of College: Students Speak Their Minds*. Cambridge, Mass.: Harvard University Press.

Locke, J. 1899. *Some Thoughts Concerning Education*. Ed. W. H. Payne. Boston.

Looking to the Twenty-first Century: Higher Education in Transition. 1995. The David D. Henry Lectures, 1986–93. Introduction by S. O. Ikenberry. Urbana-Champaign: University of Illinois Press.

Lucas, C. J. 1994. *American Higher Education: A History*. New York: St. Martin's Press.

Macaulay, T. B. 1972. "The London University." In *Selected Writings*, ed. J. Clive and T. Pinney, pp. 41–72. Chicago: University of Chicago Press.

Marsden, G. M. 1994. *The Soul of the University: From Protestant Establishment to Established Nonbelief*. New York: Oxford University Press.

Maugham, S. 1908. *The Magician*. New York: G. H. Doran.

McMullen, H. 2000. *American Libraries before 1876*. Westport, Conn.: Greenwood Press.

McPherson, M. S, M. O. Schapiro, and G. C. Winston. 1993. *Paying the Piper: Productivity, Incentives, and Financing in U.S. Higher Education*. Ann Arbor: University of Michigan Press.

The Modern University: Its Present Status and Future Prospects. 1994. Papers from the Sixth Kenan Convocation, April 22–24, 1993. Chapel Hill, N.C.: William Rand Kenan Jr. Charitable Trust.

Montaigne, M. 1957. *The Complete Works of Montaigne*. Trans. D. M. Frame. London: Hemish Hamilton.

Neue Horizonte in Forschung und Hochschule: Trends, Rahmenbedingungen und Chancen—New Horizons in Research and Higher Education: Trends, Constraints and Opportunities. 1996. Zweites Offenliches DAAK Symposium—Second Public GAAC Symposium. Publications of the GAAC Symposia, vol. 4 (1995). Bonn–Washington, D.C.: DAAK-GAAC.

Nevins, A. 1962. *The Origins of the Land-Grant Colleges and State Universities*. Washington, D.C.: Civil War Centennial Commission.

Newman, J. H. 1999. *The Idea of a University: Defined and Illustrated*. Washington, D.C.: Regency Publishing.

Orrill, R., ed. 1997. *Education and Democracy: Re-imagining Liberal Learning in America*. New York: College Entrance Examination Board.

Patton, R. B. 1838. "Public Libraries." *American Biblical Repository* 11: 174–87.

Pelikan, J. 1992. *The Idea of the University: A Reexamination*. New Haven, Conn.: Yale University Press.

Plato. 1992. *The Trial and Death of Socrates: Four Dialogues*. Trans. B. Jowett. New York: Dover.

Pope, A. 1950. *Essay on Man*. Ed. M. Mack. London: Methuen.

———. 1999. *The Dunciad*. Ed. V. Rumbold. New York: Longman.

Portman, D. N. 1992. *Early Reform in American Higher Education*. Foreword by A. P. Splete. Chicago: Nelson-Hall.

Proceedings of the American Revolutionary Colleges Conference on the Liberal Arts and Education for Citizenship in the Twenty-first Century, March 26–27, 1998, Dickinson College. Carlisle, Penn.: Clarke Center for the Interdisciplinary Study of Contemporary Issues.

Quincy, J. 1833. *Considerations Relative to the Library of Harvard University Respectfully Submitted to the Legislature of Massachusetts.* Cambridge, Mass.

Reuben, J. A. 1996. *The Making of the Modern University: Intellectual Transformation and the Marginalization of Morality.* Chicago: University of Chicago Press.

Ridky, J., and G. F. Sheldon. 1993. *Managing in Academics: A Health Center Model.* St. Louis: Quality Medical Publishing.

Rosenzweig, R. M. 1998. *The Political University: Policy, Politics, and Presidential Leadership in the American Research University.* Baltimore: Johns Hopkins University Press.

Rosovsky, H. 1990. *The University: An Owner's Manual.* New York: Norton.

Ruch, R. S. 2001. *Higher Ed, Inc.: The Rise of the For-Profit University.* Baltimore: John Hopkins University Press.

Rudenstine, N. L. 2001. *Pointing Our Thoughts: Reflections on Harvard and Higher Education, 1991–2001.* Foreword by H. H. Gray. Cambridge, Mass.: Harvard University.

Rudolph, F. 1962. *The American College and University: A History.* New York: Knopf.

———. 1977. *Curriculum: A History of the American Undergraduate Course of Study since 1636.* San Francisco: Jossey-Bass.

Science, Technology, and the Federal Government: National Goals for a New Era. 1993. Washington, D.C.: National Academy Press.

Sen, A. 1987. *On Ethics and Economics.* New York: Basil Blackwell.

Shapiro, H. T. 1987. *Tradition and Change: Perspectives on Education and Public Policy.* Ann Arbor: University of Michigan Press.

Shaw, G. B. 1908. *The Sanity of Art.* New York: B. R. Tucker.

———. 1911. *The Doctor's Dilemma.* London: Constable and Co.

Shelley, M. W. 1992. *Frankenstein.* Ed. J. M. Smith. Boston: St. Martin's Press.

Shils, E. 1992. "Universities: Since 1900." In *The Encyclopedia of Higher Education,* ed. B. R. Clark and G. Neave, pp. 67–79. New York: Pergamon Press.

———. 1997. *The Calling of Education: The Academic Ethic and Other Essays on Higher Education.* Ed. S. Grosby, foreword by J. Epstein. Chicago: University of Chicago Press.

Shires, M. A. 1996. *The Future of Public Undergraduate Education in California.* Santa Monica, Calif.: RAND.

171

Sophocles. 1994. *Antigone—The Women of Trachis—Philoctetes—Oedipus at Colonus*. Ed. and trans. H. Lloyd-Jones. Cambridge, Mass.: Harvard University Press.

Spencer, H. 1900. *Education: Intellectual, Moral, and Physical*. New York: Appleton.

Swift, J. 2003. *Gulliver's Travels*. London: Penguin.

Sykes, C. J. 1988. *ProfScam: Professors and the Demise of Higher Education*. Washington, D.C.: Regnery Gateway.

Tappan, H. 1851. *University Education*. New York: George P. Putnam.

Ticknor, G. 1876. *Life, Letters and Journals of George Ticknor*. Boston: J. R. Osgood.

Tolstoy, L. 1977. "Hadji Murat." In *Master and Man and Other Stories*, pp. 127ff. London: Penguin Classics.

Trow, M. A. 1975. "The Public and Private Lives of Higher Education." *Daedalus* 104, no. 1: 113–27.

———. 1989. "American Higher Education: Past, Present, Future." *Studies in Higher Education* 14, no. 1: 5–22.

University of Chicago. 1997. *The Aims of Education: The College of the University of Chicago*. Chicago: University of Chicago.

Van Doren, C. 1991. *A History of Knowledge: The Pivotal Events, People, and Achievements of World History*. New York: Ballantine Books.

Veblen, T. 1993. *The Higher Learning in America*. New Brunswick, N.J.: Transaction, 1993.

Veysey, L. R. 1965. *The Emergence of the American University*. Chicago: University of Chicago Press.

Walzer, M. 1994. *Thick and Thin: Moral Argument at Home and Abroad*. Notre Dame, Ind.: University of Notre Dame Press.

Wayland, F. 1842. *Thoughts on the Present Collegiate System in the U.S.* Boston: Gould, Kendall, and Lincoln.

———. 1850. "Report to the Corporation of Brown University on Changes in the System of Collegiate Education." Providence, R.I., Mar. 28.

Wells, H. G. 1993. *The Island of Doctor Moreau*. Ed. B. Alders. London: J. M. Dent.

Whitehead, A. N. 1929. *The Aims of Education*. New York: Macmillan.

Wilson, J. F. 1982. *Religion: A Preface*. Englewood Cliffs, N.J.: Prentice Hall.

Wingspread Group on Higher Education. 1993. *An American Imperative: Higher Expectations for Higher Education. An Open Letter to Those Concerned with the American Future.* Racine, Wis.: Johnson Foundation.

Wolfle, D. 1972. *The Home of Science: The Role of the University.* New York: McGraw-Hill.

Ziolkowski, T. 2000. *The Sin of Knowledge.* Princeton, N.J.: Princeton University Press.

❖ Index ❖

179